Photograph by Alexander Liberman,
Spring 1964.

ROBERT MOTHERWELL

with selections from the artist's writings

by Frank O'Hara

The Museum of Modern Art, New York

Distributed by Doubleday & Company, Inc., Garden City, New York

Trustees of The Museum of Modern Art

Acknowledgments

I wish to thank first and foremost Robert Motherwell. His generosity as a lender and his willingness to reserve certain major recent paintings for their first public showing add, I hope, a special excitement to the exhibition. His unflagging cooperation with information and patience with seemingly endless details have made it possible to provide a catalogue somewhat more intimate than usual in its factual and visual content, imparting a sense of the particular milieu of one artist's development and position in our complicated times. I am especially grateful for the "Letter from the Artist." During his return trip from Europe and prompted by the wish to make a minor correction in the catalogue, Motherwell in this letter goes on to reveal in a specific way the spontaneous and associative character of the workings of his art and thought, social as well as aesthetic, and gives us further insight into his enthusiasms and rejections.

Helen Frankenthaler has given me untiring assistance whenever called upon, combining the objectivity of the artist with the concern of a friend, and I am most thankful.

My thanks go also to Mrs. Renée Sabatello Neu for her invaluable collaboration and assistance in every phase of the exhibition from inception to installation, and to Wilder Green, who designed the installation. Waldo Rasmussen's enthusiasm for the project of a Motherwell exhibition for our museum and a subsequent tour of Europe aided immeasurably in its realization. Bryan Robertson, Director of The Whitechapel Gallery in London, where the exhibition will be shown in 1966, has given me valuable information, both in conversation and in documentation as a result of his research on a forthcoming monograph on the artist.

In preparing the catalogue, I am grateful to Kynaston McShine for compiling the first definitive chronology specifically authorized by the artist, and one which contributes valuable information on the events, associations and attitudes of our artistic period in general; to William Berkson for assistance in selecting and editing the artist's writings; to Bernard Karpel for his selective bibliography; to Miss Helen Franc for her astute editorial advice, and Jerry Matherly for editorial supervision; to Miss Françoise Boas for supervising the production of the catalogue, and Miss Mary Ahern and Joseph Del Valle for its layout and cover design, respectively.

I should also like to thank Miss Kathleen Haven for designing the invitation, announcement and poster for the exhibition.

On behalf of The Museum of Modern Art, I express gratitude to the following lenders who have provided special assistance in producing the catalogue: Mr. and Mrs. Gardiner Hempel, Mr. and Mrs. William C. Janss, The Lannan Foundation, and The Marlborough-Gerson Gallery Inc.; as well as to all the other lenders listed on page 96. Their generous consideration for the artist and his work have made possible this exhibition and its European tour under the auspices of the Museum's International Council.

F. O'H.

Contents

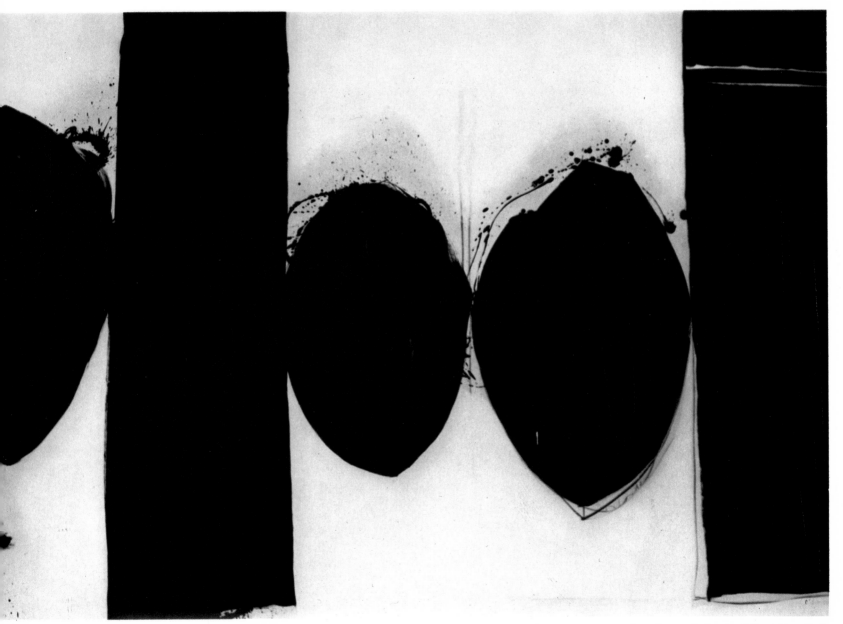

Elegy to the Spanish Republic C. 1963. Oil on canvas, 84 x 240". Collection the artist, courtesy of Marlborough-Gerson Gallery, New York.

A symbolic tale of our times, comparable to the legend of Apelles' leaving his sign on the wall, is that of the modern artist who, given the wrappings from issues of a foreign review by a friend, transforms them into two collage masterpieces; and who, given a stack of Japan paper, makes six drawings and on seeing them the next day is so excited by the black ink having bled into orange at its edges that he decides to make six hundred more drawings. The collages are *N.R.F. Numbers One and Two,* the drawings are the group called "Lyric Suite," and the artist is Robert Motherwell. Does art choose the artist, or does the man choose art?

Motherwell's choice is one of the most fascinating in modern art. As a young man of twenty-five, a university student who majored in philosophy, he decided to devote himself completely to painting, a decision which at the time held promise of little but hard work and probable discouragement. Yet, a few short years later, he was to find himself one of the leading figures in the greatest revolution in modern art since cubism, abstract expressionism.

Recently, in a television interview, Robert Motherwell remembered the aims of the early period of abstract expressionism as being "really quite simple in a way, almost too simple, considering what has happened in the last twenty years. But really I suppose most of us felt that our passionate allegiance was not to American art or in that sense to any national art, but that there was such a thing as modern art: that it was essentially international in character, that it was the greatest painting adventure of our time, that we wished to participate in it, that we wished to plant it here, that it would blossom in its own way here as it had elsewhere, because beyond national differences there are human similarities that are more consequential . . ." (bibl. 36).

The measure of the success of the abstract expressionist artists may be gauged by our response to the movement's ethical stand— today it seems an inevitable development, it is surrounded by an atmosphere of "of course." But in the late '30s and early '40s there was violent resistance to this "passionate allegiance." We forget, in the complexity of our present worldwide artistic and political engagements, that period's artistic and political isolationism (how controversial then were Gertrude Stein and Wendell Willkie!), the mania for the impressionist masters, the conviction, where there was any interest at all, that avant-garde was not only a French word but an Ecole de Paris monopoly. But the greatest resistance of all came from other American painters—the regionalists, the social realists and the traditionalists.

No account of the period can ignore Motherwell's role as an internationalist. In a sense a turn toward both revolution and internationalism were in the air, for the various national financial depressions had united most of the Western countries in crisis, if not in political agreement. And the artists, like the philosophers and the religious, had been the least economically valued members of distressed societies.

Without transition the struggle against Depression conditions became the struggle against War. War on such a scale that "conditions" became an obsolete word, faced down by the appalling actual and philosophical monolith of historical event. But the artists were not faced down by the war vocabulary. With the advent of war a heterogeneous number of American artists whose only common passion was the necessity of contemporary art's being Modern began to emerge as a movement which, in Boris Pasternak's famous description of a far different emergency, as he relates in his autobiography *Safe Conduct,* ". . . turned with the same side towards the times, stepping forward with its first declaration about its learning, its philosophy and its art."

Underlying, and indeed burgeoning within, every great work of the abstract expressionists, whether subjectively lyrical as in Gorky, publicly explosive as in de Kooning, or hieratical as in Newman, exists the traumatic consciousness of emergency and crisis experienced as personal event, the artist assuming responsibility for being, however accidentally, alive here and now. Their gift was for a somber and joyful art: somber because it does not merely reflect but sees what is about it, and joyful because it is able to exist. It is just as possible for art to look out at the world as it is for the world to look at art. But the abstract expressionists were frequently the first violators of their own gifts; to this we often owe the marvelously demonic, sullen or mysterious quality of their work, as they moved from the pictorial image to the hidden subject.

Motherwell's special contribution to the American struggle for modernity was a strong aversion to provincialism, both political and aesthetic, a profound immersion in modern French culture (especially School of Paris art and the poetry and theories of the Symbolist and Surrealist poets—conquest by absorption, like the Chinese), and a particular affinity for what he has sometimes called "Mediterranean light," which in his paintings seems to mean a mingling of the light of the California of his childhood with that of Mexico and the South of France. This affinity may explain somewhat the ambiguity between the relatively soft painted edges of many of his forms and the hard, clear contour they convey, especially in the series of "Elegies to the Spanish Republic." He can employ a rough, spontaneous stroke while evoking from the picture plane with great economy a precise personal light. There is no atmospheric light in his paintings; if he uses grey it is never twilight or dawn. One of his important early paintings is called *Western Air* (page 13) and the light in it persists in many later works.

Motherwell must have shown a surprisingly early talent for art, considering that at eleven he was awarded a fellowship to the Otis Art Institute in Los Angeles (where Philip Guston also studied briefly). Although he also attended art school at seventeen, he was not to make the final decision to devote himself to painting until 1941. The intervening years had been spent largely in the study of liberal arts and philosophy. He was led by his admiration of Delacroix's paintings to choose for his thesis subject at Harvard the aesthetic theories expounded in Delacroix's journals. On the advice of his teachers, he therefore spent the year 1938-39 in France. Delacroix led to Baudelaire, Baudelaire to the theories of the French Symbolists and especially Mallarmé, and there followed a close study of the Parisian painters.

Shortly after Motherwell's return to the United States he moved to New York. He discussed his first days there in a recent talk at the Yale University Art School:

"One of the great good fortunes I have had in my life, and there have been several, was that at a certain crucial moment in my life when I was in my mid-twenties and still hadn't really decided what I wanted to do, though in another way I'd always wanted to be a painter but through the circumstances of fate had never known a modernist one . . . for better or worse, I don't know—at a certain moment through a contact with a friend who is now professor of music at Brandeis University I decided to go to New York . . . and study with Meyer Schapiro. In those days there was nothing like there is here, that if you were interested in contemporary art there was a place where you could go and be oriented. . . . The closest approach to it, though he is essentially a classical scholar, essentially devoted to the premises of art history and so on, in those days was Meyer Schapiro. And I went to New York and studied with Schapiro. Also by chance took a room near him and knew nobody in New York —nearly died of loneliness, at how hard and cold and overwhelming it seemed to me as a person from the Far West, which is with all its defects a somewhat more casual and open place.

"And sometimes at eleven o'clock in the night I would drag the latest picture I had been making on the side in the most amateurish way around to Schapiro. And one day in exasperation really, because I had then no conception of how busy people are in New York, he said, 'It takes me two hours to tell you as best I can what any painter colleague could tell you in ten minutes. You really should know some artists.' And I said, Well, I agree . . . but I don't know any.'" (bibl. 38)

As a child, Motherwell was haunted by the fear of death, perhaps partially because of his asthmatic attacks. He grew up during the Great Depression and, no matter what one's circumstances, one could not help being affected by it. The first foreign political event to engage his feelings was the Spanish Civil War, that perfect mirror of all that was confused, venal and wrong in national and international politics and has remained so. For a slightly younger generation than Motherwell's, and by slightly I mean only by ten years or so, World War II was simply part of one's life. One went to war at seventeen or eighteen and that was what one did, perfectly simple, and one thought about it while one was about it, or you might say, in it. But Motherwell's ethical and moral considerations were already well formed by the time that war broke out, and for him the problems were quite different and also far more shattering psychologically.

It is no wonder then that when Meyer Schapiro introduced him to the European refugee artists who had fled here from the Fall of France, he was strongly drawn to them, both as emblems of art and also as emblems of experience—an experience which no American artist save Gertrude Stein suffered as the French themselves did. Their insouciant survival in the face of disaster, partly through character, partly through belief in art, is one of the great legends, and it did not escape him. To recall the presence of these artists is indeed staggering (see page 74). Motherwell's affinity for French Symbolist and Surrealist aesthetics made him a quick liaison between the refugees and certain New York artists whom he scarcely knew at the time. The capitulation of France had brought about an intense Francophilism among all liberal intellectuals, especially those who felt strongly about the tragedy of the Spanish Civil War; and the fate of Great Britain was still in question. It was not too difficult to feel a strong identification, and of course these artists were already heroes of the modern artistic revolution; if some of them hadn't invented it, they had certainly aided, abetted and extended it. In the artistic imagination these refugees represented everything valuable in modern civilization that was being threatened by physical extermination. It had never been more clear that a modern artist stands for civilization.

Modern artists ideologically, as the Jews racially, were the chosen enemies of the authoritarian states because their values were the most in opposition, so that one had a heightened sense, beyond the artistic, of seeing a Lipchitz or a Chagall walk free on the streets of New York. It is impossible for a society to be at war without each responsible element joining the endeavor, whether military, philo-sophical or artistic, and whether consciously or not. The perspectives may be different, but the temper of the time is inexorable and demanding for all concerned. I think that it was the pressure of this temper and this time that forced from abstract expressionism its statement of values, which is, and probably shall remain, unique in the history of culture. While the other protesting artistic voices of the time were bound by figuration and overt symbolism, the abstract expressionists chose the open road of personal responsibility, naked nerve-ends and possible hubris, and this separated them from the surrealists, the Mexican School and the American social realists. Belief in their personal and ethical responses saved them from aestheticism on the one hand and programmatic contortion on the other. Abstract expressionism for the first time in American painting insisted upon an artistic identity. This, of course, is what made abstract expressionism so threatening to other contemporaneous tendencies then, and even now. The abstract expressionists decided, instead of imitating the style of the European moderns, to do instead what they had done, to venture into the unknown, to give up looking at reproductions in *Verve* and *Cahiers d'Art* and to replace them with first-hand experimentation. This was the great anguish of the American artists. They had a sound theoretical, but no practical, knowledge of the suffering involved in being extreme; but they would learn. They shot off in every direction, risking everything. They were never afraid of having a serious idea, and the serious idea was never self-referential. Theirs was a struggle as ultimate as their painting. A struggle which, in the poet Edwin Denby's description in his reminiscence of the '30s, was against "... the cliché about downtown painting in the depression—the accepted idea that everybody had doubts and imitated Picasso and talked politics. None of these features seemed to me remarkable at the time, and they don't now. Downtown everybody loved Picasso then, and why not. But what they painted made no sense as an imitation of him. For myself, something in his steady wide light reminded me then of the light in the streets and lofts we lived in. At that time Tchelitchew was the uptown master, and he had a flickering light."

Spanish Painting with the Face of a Dog. (1958). Oil on muslin, 37⅛ x 75¼". Collection Mr. and Mrs. Gifford Phillips, Washington, D.C.

Spanish Prison (Window). 1943-44. Oil on canvas, 52¼ x 42¼". Collection Mrs.H. Gates Lloyd, Haverford, Pennsylvania.

View From a High Tower. 1944. Collage and oil, sight: 29¼ x 29¼". Collection Paul Peters, New York.

Mallarmé's Swan. 1944-47. Collage, sight: 43⅝ x 35⅜". Contemporary Collection of The Cleveland Museum of Art, Cleveland, Ohio. (The title is from a poem by Paul Eluard.)

Western Air. 1946-47. Oil on canvas, 72 x 54". The Museum of Modern Art, New York.

Pancho Villa, Dead and Alive. 1943. Gouache and oil with collage on cardboard, 28 x 35⅞". The Museum of Modern Art, New York.

During this period Motherwell veered between the opposite poles of the marvelous and the somber, if not morbid; from *Mallarmé's Swan*, imaged in subtle glacial beauty, to Pancho Villa's corpse, hanging bullet-riddled beside his live image, in which pink stains take on the aspect of not-yet-dried blood. Shortly before, in 1941, at the beginning of his painting career he had done three divergent pictures—*La belle méxicaine* (of his first wife, a Mexican actress), an imaginary landscape, *The Red Sun,* and the more purely conceptualized *The Little Spanish Prison.* The first owes a great deal to Picasso, the second (page 96) to the surrealist theory of automatism and especially to Masson, and the third (page 16) is connected in my mind to the royal House of Orange, a modern version of Dutch clarity of tone allied with Spanish reserve and elegance. As a self-taught painter, Motherwell had many avenues open to him, and in beginning he did not close any of them off as possibilities.

Certain of the abstract expressionists seem to have burst into paint with an already emergent personal force from the very first works we know—one thinks particularly of Motherwell and of Barnett Newman. The variety from period to period in each of these artists encompasses a broadening of technical resources, as it does in Rothko also, and moves in a steadily rising power of emotional conviction. They have had a conviction, if not a style, from the beginning, more ethical than visual, which has left them free to include anything useful and has guided them away from the peripheral. As has Clyfford Still, for example, each has chosen on several occasions to make moral statements in relation to his art, rather than aesthetic ones.

This is, of course, a matter of temperament. The passions of others of their colleagues have led to far more abrupt and dramatic changes. Motherwell once remarked that an artist is known as much by what he will *not* permit as by what he includes in the painting. One would be hard put to aver whether Newman or Pollock, de Kooning or Rothko, was more *drastic* in his decision between the Dionysian and Apollonian modes of feeling, between seething impasto excitation and somber, subtly evoked grandeur.

The Elegy. 1948. Collage, sight: 29½ x 23½". Fogg Art Museum, Harvard University, Cambridge, Massachusetts, Louise E. Bettens Fund.

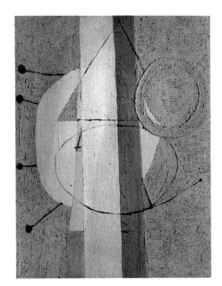

Figuration. 1945. Oil on canvas, 18¼ x 14⅛". Collection Mr. and Mrs. Gifford Phillips, Washington, D.C.

The Little Spanish Prison. 1941-44. Oil on canvas, 27⅛ x 17". Collection the artist.

Viva. 1946. Oil and collage on canvas, 13 x 16¾". Collection Dr. Robert E. Kantor, Atherton, California.

Emperor of China. 1947. Oil on canvas, 48 x 36". The Chrysler Art Museum of Provincetown, Provincetown, Massachusetts.

The Poet. 1947. Collage, sight: 55⅝ x 39⅛". Collection Mr. and Mrs. Mark Rothko, New York.

Motherwell himself is very canny in his intuition of the relative values of these modes, as they apply to his expressive purposes, and of their limitations as abstract polarities for a sensibility which is modern both through intellectual act of faith and through natural inclination. The complexity of his modern aesthetic is unified by certain basic preferences which govern every period of his work and are of an almost textbook simplicity: a painting is a sheer extension, not a window or a door; collage is as much about paper as about form; the impetus for a painting or drawing starts technically from the subconscious through automatism (or as he may say "doodling") and proceeds towards the subject which is the finished work.

These basic preferences have, however, a superstructure of great variety and subtlety. Motherwell first showed at Peggy Guggenheim's gallery Art of This Century in the early '40s. The gallery chooses the artist, but the artist also chooses the gallery; for better or worse the gallery is the artist's public milieu, and in this case it was certainly for the better. Art of This Century was the headquarters in America for the militant surrealists present in New York, and it also featured importantly Kandinsky, Mondrian, van Doesburg, Hélion, as well as Baziotes, Pollock, Hofmann, Rothko, and Still, among the Americans. Motherwell thus found himself in a milieu where simultaneous passions for the work of Mondrian, Max Ernst, de Chirico, Léger and Joseph Cornell were enriching rather than confusing, joined together in time, place and enthusiasm rather than compartmentalized and classified as they would have been in most art schools of the time, if taught at all. As the youngest member of this group, Motherwell already showed a stubborn individuality and purposefulness which were to remain characteristic through the years of experimentation with motif and symbol that lay ahead. In the preface to Motherwell's first exhibition, James Johnson Sweeney remarked on the artist's thinking ". . . directly in the materials of his art. With him, a picture grows, not in the head, but on the easel— from a collage, through a series of drawings, to an oil. A sensual interest in materials comes first." (bibl. 142, page 91)

This sensual interest in materials has led the artist away from the easel towards the small, decisively executed paper works of the *Lyric Suite* series and towards the monumental canvases, murals really, such as *Black on White, Africa,* and *Dublin in 1916, with Black and Tan.* Motherwell's admiration, which has continued throughout his career, for Matisse and Picasso, especially the "steady wide light" of which Edwin Denby wrote, have led him to a clarification of form and a toughness of drawing and color which would be impossible without the hard scrutiny of this light. It is important to differentiate the light in different painters. The distinction is not always historical, nor is it always about source. It is in its actuality the most spiritual element, technical only in so far as it requires *means,* painterly means, to appear at all. It is the summation of an artist's conviction and an artist's reality, the most revealing statement of his identity, and its emergence appears through form, color, and painterly technique as a preconceptual quality rather than an effect.

Motherwell once mentioned his experience as a child of being thrilled when a teacher drew in colored chalks a schema of the daily weather—an orange sun with yellow rays for fair weather, a purple ovoid cloud with blue strokes slanting through it for rain. Later, he remembered this experience, much as one remembers in adulthood having been pleased by Blake's *Songs of Innocence* as a child, only to find that they are masterpieces even to adults. Perhaps his belief in the communicative powers of schemata stems from this childhood experience. At any rate, his sensuality is involved as strongly with schemata as it is with texture or color. The sexual atmosphere of *Two Figures with Cerulean Blue Stripe* (page 52), for example, has a specific tenderness and a poignancy which has nothing to do with "figure" painting or with handling; it is dependent on the direct diagrammatic relation in a pictorial sense of the two forms, where the blue stripe is a curtain drawn away from the intimacy of the scene. It is the opposite of the Balthus painting of the gnome drawing the curtain from the nude girl's window—where a surrealist voyeurism gives that painting piquancy, in the Motherwell a Courbet-like health establishes a sense of both sexuality and repose.

Motherwell has also, through the same preoccupation with material, been closely involved with "series" of paintings—in quotes because the series sense is not necessarily that of subject matter but of sensitivity to findings in the motif which yield further discoveries in the material. The motif for the Elegies was discovered while he was decorating a page of a poem by Harold Rosenberg in 1948 (page 76). Almost immediately the motif appears in a Spanish context, related to Lorca's poetry: *At Five in the Afternoon, Granada;* and then shifts to the more specific associations embodied in the "Elegies to the Spanish Republic." Sometimes the motif itself dictates how to use the medium, where to drag it, splash it, flatten an intervening area or flow it, in order to accomplish the presentation of the relationship of the images as a whole experience. The range of technical procedure between *Elegy LVII* (page 66) with its almost expressionistic drama to the strict, flat statement of *Elegy LV* (page 47) reveals the fecundity Motherwell has found in this motif and also indicates his ability to bridge the gap between action painting and what Clement Greenberg has called the "Post-Painterly Abstractionists." The latter *Elegy* in particular is also related to the transcendent exposure of the most recent works. And always there is an absolute belief in the reality of the schema, executed with such force that individual paintings of the series have been variously interpreted as male verticals and female ovoids, as bulls' tails and testicles hung side by side on the wall of the arena after the fight, and as purist formal juxtapositions of rectangular and curvilinear forms. As with the great recent painting *Africa,* the possibility of the schema's arousing such a broad range of associations, depending on the emotional vocabulary of the viewer, is a sign of its power to communicate human passion in a truly abstract way, while never losing its specific identity as a pictorial statement. The exposure is one of sensibility, rather than of literal imagistic intent, and therefore engages the viewer in its meaning rather than declaring it. *(contd. on page 23)*

The Homely Protestant. (1948). Oil on composition board, 96 x 48". Collection the artist

The Joy of Living. 1943. Collage, sight: 43½ x 35¼". The Baltimore Museum of Art, Baltimore, Maryland, Saidie A. May Collection.

Collage in Beige and Black. 1944. Collage on cardboard, 43⅜ x 29⅛. Collection Ivan von Auw, Jr., New York.

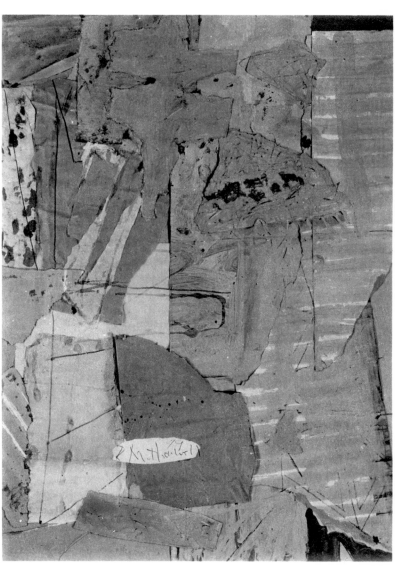

In Grey with Parasol. 1947. Oil and collage on board, sight: 47½ x 35½". The Art Gallery of Toronto, Toronto, Canada.

Collage (In Yellow and White With Torn Elements). 1949. Collage, sight: 47⅜ x 35½". Collection Mr. and Mrs. Ben Heller, New York.

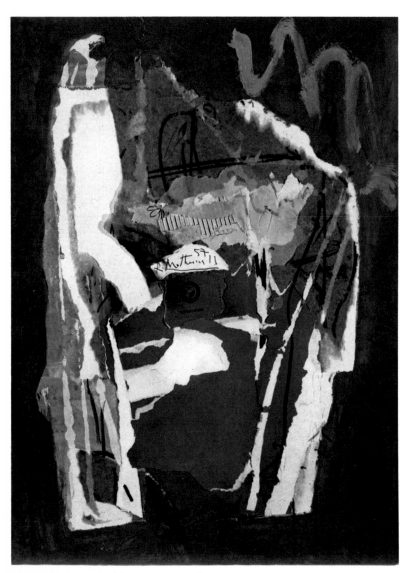

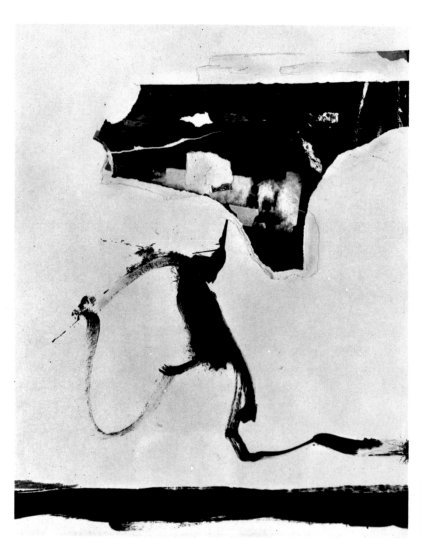

White Collage with Black Stripe. 1960. Collage, sight: 28⅜ x 22½". Collection J. Daniel Weitzman, New York.

The Tearingness of Collaging. 1957. Collage, sight: 29⅝ x 21⅜". Collection Mr. and Mrs. Max M. Zurier, Beverly Hills, California.

This is an extreme divergence in aim from other abstract expressionists, excepting Rothko, Newman and Gottlieb, while the compulsive urgency and crudity of Motherwell's drawing in paint separates him even from the latter artists. His work poises itself on the razor's edge of rawness and elegance, of brutality and refinement. With this pressure constantly on the hand, the arm, the eye, he must constantly re-invent the occasion for creation.

As devoted to exploration of motif as many of his contemporaries, he seems never to have to avoid repetition—indeed, he seems almost incapable of it. To recognize this quality in his temperament one need only compare the sensibilities involved in the *Femmes d'Algers* variations of Picasso and the "Blast" series of Gottlieb, for example, with Motherwell's series of "Elegies to the Spanish Republic." Without making a qualitative judgment, one may say that Picasso and Gottlieb are able to achieve their visual explorations within the hierarchy of an important and persuasively established pictorial structure; whereas Motherwell from *At Five in the Afternoon* (1949; page 36) on, is fighting an over-dominant and already clarified symbolic structure from which, through the years, he will wrench with astonishing energy some of the most powerful, self-exacerbating and brutally ominous works of our time, and some of the most coldly disdainful ones as well (emptying of Self). In this sense, Motherwell creates the structure that opposes him, the domination of which he must overcome to remain an artist—it is not, as with Arshile Gorky, the marvelous finding of an apparently infinite number of family forms which may be juggled and tensed for more or less specific narrative purposes. In Motherwell the family of forms is a relatively small one and the plastic handling of them carries the burden of intention, whether passionate or subtle, whether buoyant or subdued; they are never used for narrative purposes, which is perhaps why Motherwell thinks of Gorky as a surrealist artist (bibl. 38a), so different is their approach to form. Though both stemmed from the surrealist theory of automatism, Gorky proceeded into the physiological "innards" of form and reference, while Motherwell dragged like a beast of prey his automatic findings into the neutral light of day and of society.

Another important series, and one which both advances from previous preoccupations with gesture and proceeds toward later works with calligraphic elements, such as *In Green.and Ultramarine* (page 49), is the group of works entitled "Beside the Sea." Here the motif of an abstract wave breaking into the horizon and charging above it releases a marvelous arm-energy, and the characteristic Motherwell bands below, rather than becoming indications of landscape, give the works an emblematic drive. The sea is as much a metaphor as a throw of the dice is, or the "Spanish Elegies."

Here too, as elsewhere, beginning with *Viva* (page 16) and continuing through the "Je t'aime" series (page 38), many of the works show Motherwell's literal use of calligraphy as part of the compositional meaning of the painting. In the case of the "Beside the Sea" pictures, his name is usually scrawled through one of the dark bands at the bottom to lighten the tone of the passage and to give variation and variety which balance the sharp force of the "wave" above. In almost all of Motherwell's work the use of the signature is compositional: an insistence on identity, to be sure, and also an indication of the totality of the move away from easel painting—few of the pictures are "signed" in the traditional sense, they are registered by the artist as part of his life, in a matter-of-fact pictorial way, rather coldly. Like de Kooning's, his calligraphy is so beautiful it would be a loss not to incorporate it in the picture.

Gertrude Stein gives us, in *The Autobiography of Alice B. Toklas*, some thoughts which are particularly applicable to the stance of much of Motherwell's work: "She always says that americans can understand spaniards. That they are the only two western nations that can realize abstraction. That in americans it expresses itself by disembodiedness, in literature and machinery, in Spain by ritual so abstract that it does not connect itself with anything but ritual. . . .

"Americans, so Gertrude Stein says, are like spaniards, they are abstract and cruel. They are not brutal they are cruel. They have no close contact with the earth such as most europeans have. Their materialism is not the materialism of existence, of possession, it is the materialism of action and abstraction...." This observation, published in 1933, was prophetic of the whole new movement which was about to occur in American painting and sculpture, and which indeed had already been initiated by the three abstract painted metal heads of that year by David Smith, though she could not have known it. Her insight has also a relevance to the influence of contemporary Spanish artists, from Picasso and Gonzalez to Miró, on American and European artists, and particularly to the difference of application of this influence by the Americans, as opposed to, let us say, the French and the Dutch, and to the reverberations back on recent Spanish art. Her own inclination toward automatism was similar to that of many of the abstract expressionists: it fed and deepened a sense of structural necessity and of personal identity rather than obscuring the first and diffusing the latter, as automatism did so often with the surrealists.

(continued on page 30)

Personage with Yellow Ochre and White. 1947. Oil on canvas, 72 x 54". The Museum of Modern Art, New York, gift of Mr. and Mrs. Samuel M. Kootz.

Mark Rothko, Robert Motherwell and Bradley Walker Tomlin in the Guest House of Mr. and Mrs. John D. Rockefeller 3rd, 1951. The paintings are Rothko's *Number 18, 1948,* Motherwell's *The Voyage* (1949) and Tomlin's *Number 9: In Praise of Gertrude Stein* (1950).

The Voyage. (1949). Oil and tempera on paper mounted on composition board, 48 x 94". The Museum of Modern Art, New York, gift of Mrs. John D. Rockefeller 3rd.

Studio view of *Iberia #2.* 1958. Oil on canvas, 47⅛ x 80¼". The middle painting on the right is *Two Figures #11.* 1958. Oil on board, 8⅝ x 10⅝". Both collection of the artist.

Wall Painting with Stripes. 1944. Oil on canvas, 54 x 67⅛. Collection J. Patrick Lannan, Chicago, Illinois.

A View #1. 1958. Oil on canvas, 81⅛ x 104". Collection John Murray Cuddihy, New York.

The Black Sun. 1959. Oil on paper, sight: 28½ x 22½". Collection the artist, courtesy of the Marlborough-Gerson Gallery, New York.

Though both Picasso and Gonzalez as Parisians have had a universal influence stylistically, their full, bold, and fresh spirit has been most importantly absorbed in American art, I think, by Motherwell and David Smith, respectively. An essential caustic Spanish rigor reached these Americans in their different media, a toughness, a tenacity and wrought-iron insistence which seem to have been imparted to no one else. For them, the example of identity was stronger than the style, as the idea of automatism was stronger than the practice. Instead of inspiration, the example of Picasso gave Motherwell control in his passion, as that of Gonzalez gave Smith elegance in his ambition, both necessary qualities for the accomplishment of basically unruly artistic ends. In contrast to the surrealist painters, Motherwell does not yield to the subconscious, he is informed by it.

And this requires the daily confrontation of ethical as well as plastic purposes. There can be no prefigured beauty to be achieved and no predetermined set of symbolic referents which have not to be re-examined and tested for validity with each facing of the canvas. The constant testing and retesting of pictorial meaning, of the "charge" of imagery, has led to an enormous variety of content from work to work, and it has also led to the continual replenishment of the sources of that content, whether one calls it inspiration, inventiveness, restlessness, painterly ambition, whatever. The kind of artistic anxiety which seems to characterize Motherwell is the furthest from the kind that is debilitating. It has led him to find new skills in each period to serve the still mysterious demands of his consciousness.

Frank O'Hara

The Figure 4 on an Elegy. 1960. Oil on paper, 22⅞ x 28¾". Collection H. H. Arnason, New York.

Pyrenean Collage. (1961). Oil and collage on paper, 23 x 29". Collection Miss Helen Frankenthaler, New York.

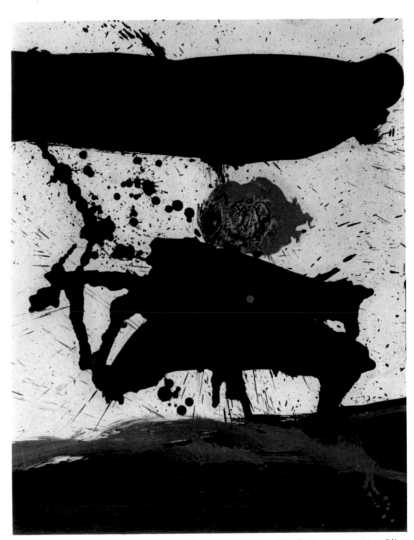

In Black with Yellow Ochre. 1961. Oil on paper, 28⅜ x 22⅜". Collection Mrs. Bliss Parkinson, New York.

Beside the Sea, #1. (1962). Oil on paper, 28⅞ x 23½".
Collection Sophie and Boris Leavitt, Hanover, Pa.

Beside the Sea, #4. (1962). Oil on paper, 28⅞ x 23".
Collection Sophie and Boris Leavitt, Hanover, Pa.

Beside the Sea, #8. 1962. Oil on paper, 28⅞ x 22¾".
Collection the artist, courtesy of Marlborough-Gerson
Gallery, New York.

Beside the Sea, #18. 1962. Oil on paper, 29 x 23".
Collection Sophie and Boris Leavitt, Hanover, Pa.

Beside the Sea, #22. 1962. Oil on paper, 28¾ x 22¾".
Collection the artist, courtesy of Marlborough-Gerson
Gallery, New York.

Beside the Sea, #24. 1962. Acrylic on paper, 28¾ x
22¾". Collection the artist, courtesy of Marlborough-
Gerson Gallery, New York.

Elegy to the Spanish Republic XXXIV. 1953-54. Oil on canvas, 80 x 100". Albright-Knox Art Gallery, Buffalo, New York, gift of Seymour H. Knox.

from: "Painter's Objects," *Partisan Review*. Winter, 1944

Now in his old age, and in a foreign country, Mondrian has assembled all his remarkable resources for purely expressive ends. In *Broadway Boogie-Woogie* the simple elements of his hitherto analytical art have been transformed. The former severe black bands are fractured into segments of color so intense in contrast that they jump, so short in segment that they become a staccato rhythm against the larger rhythms of the main structure; there are heavier, and by virtue of size (since all the colors are pure), even more intense rests; and all the while the large white background, the eternal World, reinforces the concrete and fugitive drama. For the first time a subject is present, not by virtue of its absence, but actually present, though its appearance is torn away, and only the structure bared. The Modern City! Precise, rectangular, squared, whether seen from above, below, or on the side; bright lights and sterilized life; Broadway, whites and blacks; and boogie-woogie, the underground music of the at once resigned and rebellious, the betrayed. . . . Mondrian has left his white paradise, and entered the world.

"Experience is bound to utility," as André Breton says, "and guarded by common-sense." The pleasurable "things" of other times for the most part no longer exist, and those which do no longer suffice. With what our epoch meant to replace the wonderful things of the past—the late afternoon encounters, the leisurely repasts, the discriminations of taste, the graces of manners, and the gratuitous cultivation of minds—what we might have invented, perhaps we shall never know. We have been made too busy with tasks.

At what other time could the juxtaposition of a bright square on a white ground have seemed so portentous!

The surrealists alone among modern artists refused to shift the problem to the plane of art. Ideally speaking, superrealism became a system for enhancing everyday life. True, the surrealists were always saying that "poetry should be made by all"; but they did not mean precisely what we have always meant by poetry. If they had been successful, we might not have needed "poetry" at all. Still, their various devices for finding pleasure—spiritual games, private explorations, public provocations, sensory objects, and all the rest—were

artificial enough abroad before the war. In the hard and conventional English-speaking world the devices simply could not work. Here it was the surrealists who were transformed. And it might be that their pioneer, and therefore often naive effort to enhance the life of the modern mind will be forgotten.

But in any case, it is not unimportant, this thing Alexander Calder has done, in making objects of pleasure worthy of adults [Museum of Modern Art, Calder Retrospective]. Granted, most of us must see them in museums or galleries, and that destroys half the fun. Still, there they are! The playthings of a prince for us all. . . .

It was Mondrian's influence which first led Calder from his earlier pleasantries and toys for children, to these marvelous objects for the adult mind: "I was very much moved by Mondrian's studio, large, beautiful, and irregular as it was, with the walls painted white, and divided by black lines and rectangles of bright color, like his paintings . . . and I thought at the time how fine it would be if everything there MOVED; though Mondrian himself did not approve of this idea at all." Later it came to be Miró's shapes among those of abstract artists which Calder liked best. But the essential conditions of his art remained the same; a fruitful union,—his native American ingenuity (a preference for tools, rather than the brush), leading in turn to a fresh discovery (an art of motion), coupled with the advances of European art (abstract forms) and European thought (the surrealist understanding of the desirability of the object of pleasure). The consequence of this union is that Calder's native American gifts become interesting to general culture.

There is something splendid about the form of motion, or, more exactly, motion formed; and it is with this that Calder has enchanted us.

Certain individuals represent a young generation's artistic chances. There are never many such individuals in a single field, such as painting—perhaps a hundred to begin with. The hazards inherent in man's many relations with reality are so great—there is disease and premature death; hunger and alcoholism and frustration; the historical moment may turn wrong for painters: it most often does; the young artist may betray himself, consciously or not, or may be betrayed—

from: Statement in *Fourteen Americans*. New York, Museum of Modern Art, 1946

the hazards are so great that not more than five out of a whole young generation are able to develop to the end. And for the most part it is the painting of mature men which is best.

The importance of the one-man show of young Jackson Pollock (Art of This Century) lies just in this, that he represents one of the younger generation's chances. There are not three other young Americans of whom this could be said. In his exhibit Pollock reveals extraordinary gifts: his color sense is remarkably fine, never exploited beyond its proper role; and his sense of surface is equally good. His principal problem is to discover what his true subect is. And since painting is his thought's medium, the resolution must grow out of the process of his painting itself.

In the art schools they say that one ought to learn anatomy, and then "forget" it, in the sense no doubt that for Mozart the sonata form became as much a part of the functioning of his body-mind as his personal talent. Medical anatomy is irrelevant to the ends of modern art; but there are some things that must be known as well as anatomy has been in the past, so that in the process of working in terms of feeling they need not be consciously thought. One is to know that art is not national, that to be merely an American or a French artist is to be nothing; to fail to overcome one's initial environment is never to reach the human. Still, we cannot become international by willing it, or by following a foreign pattern. This state of mind arises instead from following the nature of true reality, by taking things for what they are, whether native or foreign. It is part of what Plato meant by *techne,* that is, mobilizing one's means in relation to an insight into the structure of reality. With such insight, nationalities become accidental appearances; and no rendering of the appearance of reality can move us like a revelation of its structure. Thus when we say that one of the ideals of modern art has been internationalism, it is not meant in the sense of a slogan, of a super-chauvinism, but as a natural consequence of dealing with reality on a certain level.

At Five in the Afternoon. 1949. Casein on cardboard, 15 x 20". Collection the artist.

from: "Beyond the Aesthetic," *Design*. April, 1946

For the goal which lies beyond the strictly aesthetic the French artists say the "unknown" or the "new," after Baudelaire and Rimbaud; Mondrian used to say "true reality." "Structure" or "gestalt" may be more accurate: reality has no degrees nor is there a "super" one (*surréalisme*). Still, terminology is unimportant. Structures are found in the interaction of the body-mind and the external world; and the body-mind is active and aggressive in finding them. As Picasso says, there is no use looking at random: to find is the thing.

The aesthetic is the sine qua non for art: if a work is not aesthetic, it is not art by definition. But in this stage of the creative process, the strictly aesthetic—which is the sensuous aspect of the world—ceases to be the chief end in view. The function of the aesthetic instead becomes that of a medium, a means for getting at the infinite background of feeling in order to condense it into an object of perception. We feel through the senses, and everyone knows that the content of art is feeling; it is the creation of an object for sensing that is the artist's task; and it is the qualities of this object that constitute its felt content. Feelings are just how things feel to us; in the old-fashioned sense of these words, feelings are neither "objective" nor "subjective," but both, since all "objects" or "things" are the result of an interaction between the body-mind and the external world. "Body-mind" and "external world" are themselves sharp concepts only for the purposes of critical discourse, and from the standpoint of a stone are perhaps valid but certainly unimportant distinctions. It is natural to rearrange or invent in order to bring about states of feeling that we like, just as a new tenant refurnishes a house.

The passions are a kind of thirst, inexorable and intense, for certain feelings or felt states. To find or invent "objects" (which are, more strictly speaking, relational structures) whose felt quality satisfies the passions—that for me is the activity of the artist, an activity which does not cease even in sleep. No wonder the artist is constantly placing and displacing, relating and rupturing relations; his task is to find a complex of qualities whose feeling is just right—

veering toward the unknown and chaos, yet ordered and related in order to be apprehended.

The activity of the artist makes him less socially conditioned and more human. It is then that he is disposed to revolution. Society stands against anarchy; the artist stands for the human against society; society therefore treats him as an anarchist. Society's logic is faulty, but its intimation of an enemy is not. Still, the social conflict with society is an incidental obstacle in the artist's path.

It is Cézanne's feeling that determined the form of his pictorial structure. It is his pictorial structure that gives off his feeling. If all his pictorial structures were to disappear from the world, so would a certain feeling.

The sensation of physically operating on the world is very strong in the medium of the papier collé or collage, in which various kinds of paper are pasted to the canvas. One cuts and chooses and shifts and pastes, and sometimes tears off and begins again. In any case, shaping and arranging such a relational structure obliterates the need, and often the awareness, of representation. Without reference to likenesses, it possesses feeling because all the decisions in regard to it are ultimately made on the grounds of feelings.

Feelings must have a medium in order to function at all; in the same way, thought must have symbols. It is the medium, or the specific configuration of the medium that we call a work of art that brings feeling into being, just as do responses to the objects of the external world. Apart from the struggle to endure—as Spinoza says, substance is no stronger than its existence—the changes that we desire in the world, public or private are in the interest of feeling. The medium of painting is such changing and ordering on an ideal plane, ideal in that the medium is more tractable, subtle, and capable of emphasis (abstraction is a kind of emphasis) than everyday life.

Drama moves us: conflict is an inherent pattern in reality. Harmony moves us too: faced as we are with ever imminent disorder. It is a powerful ideal. Van Gogh's drama and Seurat's silent harmony

Je t'aime IIa. 1955. Oil on canvas, 71⅞ x 53¼". Collection Mr. and Mrs. I. Donald Grossman, New York.

Je t'aime IV. 1955-57. Oil on canvas, 70⅛ x 100″. Collection Mr. and Mrs. Walter Bareiss, Munich, Germany.

were born in the same country and epoch: but they do not contradict one another; they refer to different patterns among those which constitute reality. In them the projection of the human has become so desocialized as to take on the aspect of the unknown. Yet what seems more familiar when we confront it?

The "pure" red of which certain abstractionists speak does not exist no matter how one shifts its physical contexts. Any red is rooted in blood, glass, wine, hunter's caps, and a thousand other concrete phenomena. Otherwise we should have no feeling toward red or its relations, and it would be useless as an artistic element.

But the most common error among the whole-hearted abstractionists nowadays is to mistake the medium for an end in itself, instead of a means.

On the other hand, the surrealists erred in supposing that one can do without a medium, that in attacking the medium one does not destroy just one means for getting into the unknown. Color and space relations constitute such a means because from them can be made structures which exhibit the various patterns of reality.

Like the cubists before them, the abstractionists felt a beautiful thing in perceiving how the medium can, of its own accord, carry one into the unknown, that is to the discovery of new structures. What an inspiration the medium is. Colors on the palette or mixed in jars on the floor, assorted papers, or a canvas of a certain concrete space—no matter what, the painting mind is put into motion, probing, finding, completing. The internal relations of the medium lead to so many possibilities that it is hard to see how anyone intelligent and persistent enough can fail to find his own style.

Like Rimbaud before them, the surrealists abandoned the aesthetic altogether; it takes a certain courage to leave poetry for Africa. They revealed their insight as essentially moral in never forgetting for a moment that most living is a process of conforming to an established order which is inhuman in its drives and consequences. Their hatred sustained them through all the humiliating situations in which the modern artist finds himself, and led them to perceptions beyond the

reach of more passive souls. For them true "poetry" was freedom from mechanical social responses. No wonder they loved the work of children and the insane—if not the creatures themselves.

In the end one must agree with Rilke when he says that with "nothing can one touch a work of art so little as with critical words: they always come down to more or less happy misunderstandings." It was Marcel Duchamp who was critical, when he drew a moustache on the Mona Lisa. And so was Mondrian when he dreamt of the dissolution of painting, sculpture, and architecture into a transcendent ensemble.

In Brown and White. 1960. Collage, sight: 39½ x 26". Collection Mr. and Mrs. Joseph S. Iseman, New York.

from: "A Tour of the Sublime," *Tiger's Eye*. December 15, 1948

The Sublime I take to be the emphasis of a possible felt quality in aesthetic experience, the exalted, the noble, the lofty, "the echo of a great mind," as the treatise formerly ascribed to Longinus phrases it.

The history of modern art can be conceived of as a military campaign, as a civil war that has lasted more than a hundred years—if movements of the spirit can be dated—since Baudelaire first requested a painting that was to be specifically modern in subject and style. Perhaps the first dent in the lines of traditional conceptions was made by the English landscapists and by Courbet, but the major engagement begins, earlier means being now obsolete, with Manet and the Impressionists who, whatever their subjective radiance and rhythms, represent objectively the rise of modern realism (in the sense of everyday subjects), that is, the decisive attack on the Sublime. . . . The story is interesting if the essence of their goal is taken to be a passionate desire to get rid of what is dead in human experience, to get rid of concepts, whether aesthetic or metaphysical or ethical or social, that, being garbed in the costumes of the past, get in the way of their enjoyment. As though they had the sensation, while enjoying nudes in the open air, that someone was likely to move a dark Baroque decor into the background, altering the felt quality of their experience. No wonder they wanted to bury the past permanently. I pass over how remarkable it seems to some of us that small groups of men should have had, for a century or more, as one of their ideals getting rid of what is dead in human experience.

A true history of modern art will take account of its innumerable concrete rejections. True, it is more difficult to think under the aspect of negations, or to contend with what is not stated. But this does not justify the history of an indirect process being written under the category of the direct. I do not see how the works of a Mondrian or Duchamp can be described apart from the description of what they refused to do. Indeed, a painter's most difficult and far-reaching decisions revolve around his rejections.

Suppose that we assume that, despite defaults and confusions, modern art succeeded in ridding us of the costumes of the past, of kings and queens and the glory of conquerors and politicos and mountains, rhetoric and the grand, that is became, though "understood" only by a minority, a people's art, a peculiarly modern humanism, that its tactics in relation to the general human situation were those of gentle, strong and humane men defending their values with intelligence and ingenuity against the property-loving world. One ought not over-simplify: if humane men would doubtless agree with the character in Dostoievski who holds that no gain, social or military, can be equated against the life of a single child, nevertheless I take a murderer by profession like "Monsieur Verdoux" to fall under the heading of a gentle, strong and humane. . . . Indeed, without trying to present a paradox, but simply in an effort to be phenomenologically exact, and speaking apart from times of war, one might say that it is only the most inhuman professions in modern society that permit the agent to behave nicely in everyday life and to regard the world with a merry and well glassed eye.

When living Ulysses meets in Hades the shade of Ajax, from whom he had won the armor and set on the course that led to Ajax's death, Ulysses expresses his regret; but Ajax "did not answer, but went his way on into Erebus with the other wraiths of those dead and gone." One has not the right from one's anguish to bring to the surface another's anguish. This must be the meaning of the first century A.D. treatise on the Sublime when it says: "The silence of Ajax in The Wraiths is inexpressibly great." Otherwise it can only mean how terrible is being dead.

Perhaps—I say perhaps because I do not know how to reflect, except by opening my mind like a glass-bottomed boat so that I can watch what is swimming below—painting becomes Sublime when the artist transcends his personal anguish, when he projects in the midst of a shrieking world an expression of living and its end that is silent and ordered. That is opposed to expressionism. So is the beauty and perfection of the School of Paris. Like the latter, all of us must reject the Sublime in the social sense, in its association with institutional authority regardless of one's relation to beauty as an ideal. In the metaphysical sense, it cannot be a question of intent,

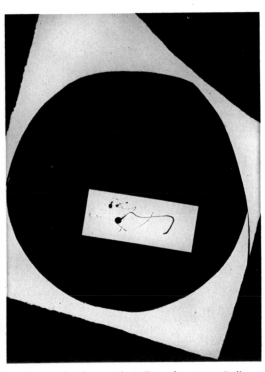

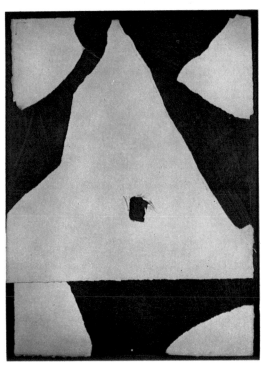

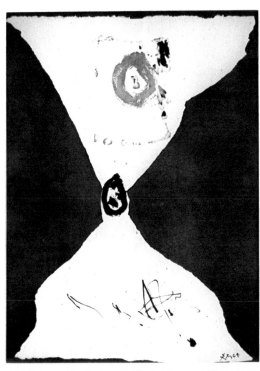

In Blue and White with Calligraphy. 1964. Collage, 30 x 22″. Collection the artist, courtesy of Marlborough-Gerson Gallery, New York.

In White with 4 Corners. 1964. Collage on cardboard, 30 x 22″. Collection the artist, courtesy of Marlborough-Gerson Gallery, New York.

In White with Pink and Black Rings. 1964. Collage, 30⅛ x 22″. Collection the artist, courtesy of Marlborough-Gerson Gallery, New York.

one experiences the Sublime or not, according to one's fate and character.

from: "On My Way," prefatory note for *Arp: "On My Way."* New York, Wittenborn, Schultz, 1948

The sky is August Blue. Green skins dangle from the wild cherry trees. Its hair scorched, the ground drowses. If an Arp sculpture were present, it too would sleep in the sun ("I work until enough of my life has flowed into its body").

from: prefatory note for *Kahnweiler: "The Rise of Cubism."* New York, Wittenborn, Schultz, 1949

Sometime in 1909 or 1910 Picasso took "the great step," as Kahnweiler puts it, and pierced the "skin" of objects, reducing them and the world in which they existed to what we would now call subjective process. With this step cubism snapped traditional naturalism. Working with great intelligence, stubbornness and objectivity, they stumbled over the leading insight of the 20th century, all thought and feeling is relative to man, he does not reflect the world but invents it. Man is his own invention; every artist's problem is to invent himself. How stupid from this point of view to pass one's time copying nature or history. And what an invention is Mozart! Through analysis and work of great objectivity, Braque and Picasso were led directly to the subjective—I am speaking of the brief period when their insight did not waver—to the problem of inventing themselves. It is in a much deeper sense than Manolo guessed when he made his crude joke that Picasso's family would not have recognized him at the Barcelona station if he had descended as a cubist portrait. Cubism invented Picasso as much as he invented Cubism; it revealed himself to himself, as painting does to every true painter; of course it made him unintelligible to others.

from: "Preliminary Notice—From Baudelaire to Surrealism," Robert Motherwell, Virginia City, Nevada, October 1949

Still, the fundamental relation between modernist painting and French poetry is indirect, pervasive, and not wholly recoverable now; but it is extraordinary how, in countries that speak other tongues, the implications of the fact that French is the language of the School of Paris are so often passed over. And do not tell me that Parisian painters have not read or conversed with poets.

True painters disdain "literature" in painting. It is an error to disdain literature itself. Plainly, painting's structure is sufficiently expressive of feelings, of feelings far more subtle and "true" to our being than those representing or reinforcing anecdotes; but true poetry is no more anecdotal than painting. Both have sought in modern times to recover the primitive, magical and bold force of their mediums and to bring it into relation to the complexities of modern felt attitudes and knowledge; no modernist painter can read in this marvelous book of some of the ideals of French poets without a sharp sense of recognition.

Perhaps, the "plasticity" that we painters so admire is no less than the poetry of visual relations.

The miners' graveyard. Beyond, the town's ruins, burnt sienna, pink, yellow ochre—arid and clear in the distance, as the hill towns of Italy. Here silent monuments of the past rest, in white October sun, wind sweeping from the Sierra Nevada mountains. Crystal light! Vertical personages gaping, a broken grave. Here, too, in the midst of gold and silver, there were yearnings for the word, but what confusions! Jenny Lind, the Great Patti, Mark Twain, General Tom Thumb, Uncle Tom's Cabin companies. As with French poets, desire for the sensuous "new." Dragged up the mountains from California in eight-span wagons, wood, to construct French baroque mansions. Glass chandeliers from Vienna. But the desert air is white, Mallarmé's swan.

from: *Black and White*. Exhibition Catalogue. New York, Samuel Kootz Gallery, 1950

There is so much to be seen in a work of art, so much to say if one is concrete and accurate, that it is a relief to deal on occasion with a simple relation.

Yet not even *it,* no more than any other relation in art, is *so* simple.

The chemistry of the pigments is interesting: ivory black, like bone black, is made from charred bones or horns, carbon black is the result of burnt gas, and the most common whites—apart from cold, slimy zinc oxide and recent bright titanium dioxide—are made from lead and are extremely poisonous on contact with the body. Being soot, black is light and fluffy, weighing a twelfth of the average pigment: it needs much oil to become a painter's paste, and dries slowly. Sometimes I wonder, laying in a great black stripe on a canvas, what animal's bones (or horns) are making the furrows of my picture. A captain on the Yukon River painted the snow black in the path of his ships for 29 miles; the black strip melted three weeks in advance of spring, and he was able to reach clear water. Black does not reflect, but absorbs all light, that is its essential nature; while that of white is to reflect all light: dictionaries define it as snow's color, and one thinks of the black slit glasses used when skiing. For the rest, there is a chapter in Moby Dick that evokes white's qualities as no painter could, except in his medium.

Wall Painting IV. 1954. Oil on canvas, 54⅛ x 72⅛". Collection Mr. and Mrs. Ben Heller, New York.

from: *For David Smith 1950*, Willard Gallery, New York, 1950

If the notion of art as being in its beginnings, of always being its beginnings, appears to be a rather general source of inspiration, still for some of us the notion is personal and real.

What remains is for each modern artist to realize the general intent in his own way. Young Smith's work, before this last decade, seemed to me to be more concerned with the beautiful; it was "abstract," harmonious, felt. Now his present work seems to me to be emotive and anguished, less "pure." But as Baziotes remarked the other day, "If Manet was the first painter to have the concept of 'pure' painting, he was also the first painter to be relatively uninterested in the outside world." David Smith is less detached; outside reality blows through him; we see it in the structure of these sculptures; his structural sense is made to correspond to his felt image of the world.

When I saw that David places his work against the mountains and sky, the impulse was plain, an ineffable desire to see his humanness related to exterior reality, to nature at least if not man, for the marvel of the felt scale that exists between a true work and the immovable world, the relation that makes both human.

Elegy to the Spanish Republic LXX. (1961). Oil on canvas, 69 x 114". Collection the artist, courtesy of Marlborough-Gerson Gallery, New York.

Elegy to the Spanish Republic LIV. 1957-1961. Oil on canvas, 70 x 90¼". The Museum of Modern Art, New York, anonymous gift.

from: "What Abstract Art Means to Me," *The Museum of Modern Art Bulletin.*
Spring 1951

The emergence of abstract art is a sign that there are still men of feeling in the world. Men who know how to respect and follow their inner feelings, no matter how irrational or absurd they may first appear. From their perspective, it is the social world that tends to appear irrational and absurd. It is sometimes forgotten how much wit there is in certain works of abstract art. There is a certain point on the curve of anguish where one encounters the comic—I think of Miró, of the late Paul Klee, of Charlie Chaplin, of what healthy and human values their wit displays.

I like the way that many Parisian painters have taken over the word "poetry" in speaking of what they value in painting. But in the English-speaking world there is usually an implication of "literary content," if one speaks of a painting as having "real poetry." Yet the word "aesthetic" does not satisfy me. Maybe because it calls up in my mind those dull classrooms and books when I was a student of philosophy and the nature of the aesthetic was a course given in the philosophy department of every university. I think now that there is no such thing as "the aesthetic," no more than there is any such thing as "art," that each period and place has its own art and its aesthetic—which are specific applications of a more general set of human values, with emphases and rejections corresponding to the basic needs and desires of a particular place and time. I think that abstract art is uniquely modern—not in the sense that word is sometimes used, that our art has "progressed" over the art of the past, though abstract art may indeed represent an emergent level of evolution, but in the sense that abstract art represents the particular acceptances and rejections of men living under the conditions of modern times. If I were asked to generalize about this condition, as it has been manifest in poets, painters and composers during the last century and a half, I should say that it is a fundamentally romantic response to modern life—rebellious, individualistic, unconventional, sensitive, irritable. I should say that these attitudes arose from a feeling of being ill at ease in the universe, so to speak—the collapse of religion, of the old close knit community and family may have something to do with the origins of the feeling. I do not know.

But whatever the source of this sense of being unwedded to the universe, I think that one's art is one's effort to wed oneself to the universe, to unify oneself through union. Sometimes I have an imaginary picture in mind of the poet Mallarmé in his study late at night —changing, blotting, transferring, transforming each word and its relations with such care—and I think that the sustained energy for the travail must have come from the secret knowledge that each word was a link in the chain that he was forging to bind himself to the universe; and so with other poets, composers and painters. If this suggestion is true, then modern art has a different face from the art of the past because it has a somewhat different function for the artist in our time.

I suppose that the art of far more ancient and "simple" artists expressed something quite different, a feeling of *already* being at one with the world. . . .

One of the most striking aspects of abstract art's appearance is her nakedness, an art stripped bare. How many rejections on the part of her artists! Whole worlds—the world of objects, the world of power and propaganda, the world of anecdotes, the world of fetishes and ancestor worship. . . .

What new kind of *mystique* is this, one might ask. For make no mistake, abstract art is a form of mysticism.

Well, this is not to think of the situation very subtly. To leave out consideration of what is being put into the painting, I mean. One might truthfully say that abstract art is stripped bare of other things in order to intensify it, its rhythms, spatial intervals, and color structure. Abstraction is a process of emphasis, and emphasis vivifies life, as A. N. Whitehead said.

Nothing as drastic an innovation as abstract art could have come into existence, save as the consequence of a most profound, relentless, unquenchable need.

The need is for felt experience—intense, immediate, direct, subtle, unified, warm, vivid, rhythmic.

from: "The Painter and the Audience," *Perspectives U.S.A.* Autumn 1954

Sometimes when I walk down Park Avenue and regard the handsome and clean-cut Lever Brothers building, which I suppose belongs to the same "family" as the tall UN skyscraper, I think to myself how the interior walls need the sensuality and moral integrity of modern painting; but then one cannot help reflecting that what lies behind this building is not the possibility of collaboration between men on "ultimate concerns," but instead big business, that is, a popular soap, whose needs in the end will determine everything, including how its makers think about reality. It is strange when a commodity is more powerful than the men who make it.

My emphasis is the absence of direct social relations between the modern painter and his audience. One can understand though it is curious to think this way, that a Picasso is regarded by speculators as a sounder investment than French Government bonds; but what a peculiar responsibility or circumstance for a solitary artist. Indeed, our society, which has seemed so freedom-giving and passive in its attitudes toward the artist really makes extraordinary demands upon him: on the one side, to be free in some vague spiritual sense, free to act only as an artist, and yet on the other side to be rigorously tested as to whether the freedom he has achieved is great enough to be more solidly dependable than a government's financial structure, as though the painter's realistic audience, as opposed to an audience with sentiment, were rare stamp collectors. No wonder that modern painters, in view of these curious relations to society, have taken art matters into their own hands, decided for themselves what its subjects are to be, and how they are to be treated. Art like love is an active process of growth and development, not a God-given talent; and since in modern society the audience rarely sees the actual process of art, the audience's remoteness from the act of painting has become so great that practically all writing about modern art has become explaining to the audience what the art is that the audience has got so far away from. And those whose profession

is to do the explaining are more often than not mistaken. It is in this context that one has to understand the fury of Picasso's famous statement of 1935 beginning, "Everyone wants to understand art. Why not try to understand the song of a bird? One loves the night flowers, everything around one, without trying to understand them. While the painting everyone must understand. If only they would realize that an artist works above all of necessity. . . ." What angers Picasso is not the desire to understand, but that understanding should pose a problem, that his audience is unprepared for him. More exactly, prepared for something else.

opposite: *Elegy to the Spanish Republic LVIII.* 1957-60. Oil on canvas, 84 x 108¾". Rose Art Museum, Brandeis University, Waltham, Massachusetts, gift of Julian J. and Joachim Jean Aberbach.

Elegy to the Spanish Republic LV. 1955-60. Oil on canvas, 70⅛ x 76⅛". Contemporary Collection of The Cleveland Museum of Art, Cleveland, Ohio.

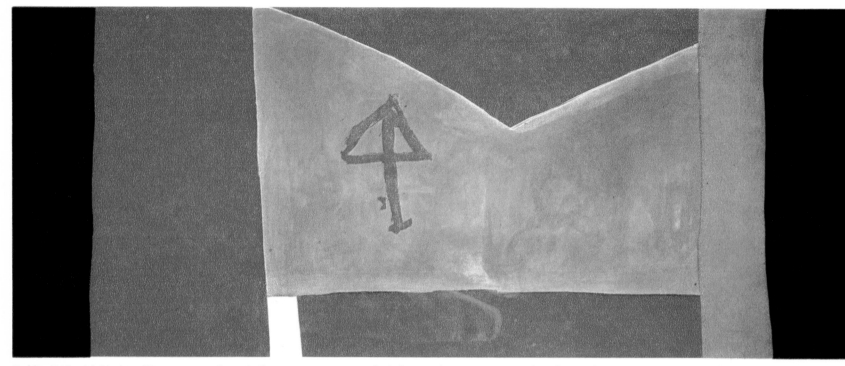

Dublin 1916, with Black and Tan. 1964. Acrylic and oil on canvas, 84⅛ x 204¼". Collection the artist, courtesy of Marlborough-Gerson Gallery, New York.

In Green and Ultramarine. 1963-65. Oil on canvas, 88 x 248½". Collection the artist, courtesy of Marlborough-Gerson Gallery, New York.

from: statement in *The New Decade* exhibition catalogue. New York, Whitney Museum & Macmillan, 1955

If a painting does not make a human contact, it is nothing. But the audience is also responsible. Through pictures, our passions touch. Pictures are vehicles of passion, of all kinds and orders, not pretty luxuries like sports cars. In our society, the capacity to give and to receive passion is limited. For this reason, the act of painting is a deep human necessity, not the production of a hand-made commodity. I respect a collector who returned one of my "abstract" pictures to the gallery, saying it was too tragic in feeling for her to be able to look at it every day. But somewhere there is a man with a tragic sense of life who loves that same picture, and I think he will find one day a way to have it. These are real human contacts, and I love painting that it can be a vehicle for human intercourse. In this solitary and apathetic society, the rituals are so often obsolete and corrupt, out of accord with what we really know and feel. . . . True painting is a lot more than "picture-making." A man is neither a decoration nor an anecdote.

from: "The Significance of Miró" by Robert Motherwell, Excerpts from *Art News*, May, 1959

I like everything about Miró—his clear-eyed face, his modesty, his ironically-edged reticence as a person, his constant hard work, his Mediterranean sensibility, and other qualities that manifest themselves in a continually growing body of work that, for me, is the most moving and beautiful now being made in Europe. A sensitive balance between nature and man's works, almost lost in contemporary art, saturates Miró's art, so that his work, so original that hardly anyone has any conception of how original, immediately strikes us to the depths. No major artist's atavism flies across so many thousands of years (yet no artist is more modern): "My favorite schools of painting are as far back as possible—the primitives. To me the Renaissance does not have the same interest." He is his own man, liking what he likes, indifferent to the rest. He is not in competition with past masters or contemporary reputations, does nothing to give his work an immortal air. His advice to young artists has been: "Work hard—and then say *merde!*" It never occurs to him to terrorize the personnel of the art-world, anxiety-ridden and insecure, as many of our contemporaries, angry and hurt, do. He believes that one's salvation is one's own responsibility, and follows his own line of grace and felt satisfaction, indifferent to others' opinions, but with his own sense of right. One might say that originality is what originates just in one's own being. He is a brave man, of dignity and modesty, passion and grace. He has the advantage of liking his own origins.

"I do not dream of a paradise, but I have a profound conviction of a society better than that in which we live at this moment, and of which we are still prisoners. I have faith in a future collective culture, vast as the seas and the lands of our globe, where the sensibility of each individual will be enlarged. Studios will be re-created like those of the Middle Ages, and the students will participate fully, each bringing his own contribution. For my part, my desire has always been to work in a team, fraternally. In America, the artisan has been killed. In Europe, we must save him. I believe that he is going to revive, with force and beauty. These past years have seen, nevertheless, a reevaluation of the artisan's means of expression: ceramics, lithos, etchings....All these objects, less dear than a picture and often as authentic in their plastic affirmation, will get around more and more. The supply can equal the demand, understanding and growth will not be restricted to the few, but for all." We feel the melancholy shadow of Franco's gloomy, suppressed Spain over his words, as well as the human desire to escape one's solitary studio that nearly every modern painter feels on occasion. But Miró must also feel, with his incredible sensitivity to the various materials of plastic art, like his peers Matisse and Picasso before him, continual inspiration in sensing out a new material, and in finding that precise image that stands at an equal point between its own nature and his own. And who would not prefer the constant company of artisans to that international café society around art that otherwise surrounds us? When he was in America twelve years ago, making a beautiful mural for a hotel in Ohio, he answered questions about how he likes to live: "Well, here in New York I cannot live life as I want to. There are too many appointments, too many people to see, and with so much going on I become too tired to paint. But when I am leading the life I like to in Paris, and even more in Spain, my daily schedule is very severe and strict and simple. At 6 A.M. I get up and have my breakfast—a few pieces of bread and some coffee—and by seven I am at work...until noon....Then lunch....By 3 I am at work again and paint without interruption until 8....*Merde!* I absolutely detest openings and nearly all parties. They are commercial, 'political,' and everyone talks so much. They give me the 'willies.' ...The sports! I have a passion for baseball. Especially the night games. I go to them as often as I can. Equally with baseball, I am mad about hockey—ice hockey, I went to all the games I could...."

His main two subjects are sexuality and metamorphosis, this last having to do with identity in differences, differences in identity to which he is especially sensitive, like any great poet. As Picasso says, painting is a kind of rhyming. Miró is filled with sexuality, warm,

abandoned, clean-cut, beautiful and above all intense—his pictures breathe eroticism, but with the freedom and grace of the Indian love-manuals. His greatness as a man lies in true sexual liberation and true heterosexuality; he has no guilt, no shame, no fear of sex; nothing sexual is repressed or described circumspectly—penises are as big as clubs, or as small as peanuts, teeth are hack-saw blades, fangs, bones, milk, breasts are round and big, small and pear-shaped, absent, double, quadrupled, mountainous and lavish, hanging or flying, full or empty, vaginas exist in every size and shape in profusion, and hair!—hair is everywhere, pubic hair, underarm hair, hair on nipples, hair around the mouth, hair on the head, on the chin, in the ears, hair made of hairs that are separate, each hair waving in the wind as sensitive to touch as an insect's antenna, hairs in every hollow that grows them, hairs wanting to be caressed, erect with kisses, dancing with ecstasy. They have a life of their own, like that Divine hair God left behind in the vomit of the whore-house in Lautréamont. Miró's torsos are mainly simplified shapes, covered with openings and protuberances—no creatures ever had so many openings to get into, or so many organs with which to do it. It is a coupling art, an art of couples, watched over by sundry suns, moons, stars, skies, seas and terrains, constantly varied and displaced, like the backgrounds in Herriman's old cartoons of Krazy Kat. But in Miró there are no dialogues. Simply the primeval energy of a universe in which everything is attracted to everything else, as visibly as lovers are, even if they are going to bite each other. In Picasso the erotic is usually idyllic, more rarely rape, and now lately old men looking in lascivious detachment at young nudes. In Miró there is constant interplay. Even his solitary figures are magnetized, tugged at by the background, spellbound by being bodies that move. It is a universe animated by the pull of feeling.

As Renaissance painters did, he proceeds by separate steps (though his process has nothing else in common with Renaissance painting, any more than does his image of reality). The whole pro-

Two Figures with Cerulean Blue Stripe. 1960. Oil on canvas, 84 x 109¼". Collection Sophie and Boris Leavitt, Hanover, Pennsylvania, courtesy of The Baltimore Museum of Art.

cess is pervaded throughout by an exquisite "purity," that is, by a concrete and sensitive love for his medium that never distorts the essential nature of the medium, but respects its every nuance of being, as one respects someone one loves. The nature of the medium can be distorted by a brutal or insensitive artist, just as a person's nature can be distorted by another human being. The painting medium is essentially a rhythmically animated, colored surface-plane that is invariably expressive, mainly of feelings—or their absence.... The expression is the result of emphasis, is constituted by what is emphasized, and, more indirectly, by what is simply assumed or ignored. In "bad" painting the emphases are essentially meaningless, i.e., not really felt, but counterfeited or aped.

from: statement made in 1957 for *The New American Painting*. Exhibition Catalogue. New York, The Museum of Modern Art, 1959

I believe that painters' judgments of painting are first ethical, then aesthetic, the aesthetic judgments flowing from an ethical context. ... Søren Kierkegaard, who did not value painting, was nevertheless very much aware of this distinction in his general analysis of existence. In quite another context, he wrote, "If anything in the world can teach man to venture it is the ethical, which teaches him to venture everything for nothing, to risk everything, and also therefore to renounce the flattery of the world-historical . . . the ethical is the absolute, and in all eternity the highest value"....Venturesomeness is only one of the ethical values respected by modern painters. There are many others, integrity, sensuality, sensitivity, knowingness, passion, dedication, sincerity, and so on which taken altogether represent the ethical background of judgment in relation to any given work of modern art.

... One has to have an intimate acquaintance with the language of contemporary painting to be able to see the real beauties of it; to see the ethical background is even more difficult. It is a question of consciousness....

Without ethical consciousness, a painter is only a decorator.

Without ethical consciousness, the audience is only sensual, one of aesthetes.

from: Philadelphia Museum Panel on "The Concept of Renew," *It Is*. Spring 1960

One might say that the specific enemies of modern art are those values that are artifically preserved, especially established institutions, which are the chief instruments for artificially preserving values. There is not a great deal of difference between the Louisiana State Legislature, the Libby Cannery, the Philadelphia Museum, the Eastman Kodak Laboratories, Cardinal Spellman's diocese, the Venetian ghetto and the Russian Writers' Congress—all are involved in preserving what is dead.

For my part, I have never met a man or experienced a work of art that I respected, without a sense of freshness emanating from either. A moral beauty of modern art, which has led it inevitably and dialectically to the new, is its inability to stand that which is musty and stale. No wonder Marcel Duchamp says he is so grateful to anyone who can show him something new! No wonder those who have a stake in the old and stale hate the new! What an ultimate confrontation!

To put the tendency of my thought in another way, I think that it is impossible to be deeply in touch with one's feelings and, looking at the world squarely, not to become revolutionary, not to want to change—in relation to imagined new possibilities—the areas of which one is aware. To create is not to repeat, but to discover, critically and radically and freshly.

54

from: "A Conversation at Lunch," *Smith College. Robert Motherwell.* Northampton, Massachusetts, January 1963

A picture is a collaboration between artist and canvas. "Bad" painting is when an artist enforces his will without regard for the sensibilities of the canvas. . . .

An artist is someone who has an abnormal sensitivity to a medium. The main thing is not to be dead. And nearly everyone is dead, painter or not. Only an alive person can make an alive expression. The problem of inspiration is simply to be fully alive at a given moment when working.

I don't exploit so-called "accidents" in painting. I accept them if they seem appropriate. There is no such thing as an "accident" really; it is a kind of casualness: it happened so let it be, so to speak. One doesn't want a picture to look "made" like an automobile or a loaf of bread in waxed paper. Precision belongs to the world of machinery—which has its own forms of the beautiful. One admires Léger. But machinery created with brush and paint is ridiculous, all the same. . . . I agree with Renoir, who loved everything hand-made.

I take an elegy to be a funeral lamentation or funeral song for something one cared about. The "Spanish Elegies" are not "political" but my private insistence that a terrible death happened that should not be forgot. They are as eloquent as I could make them. But the pictures are also general metaphors of the contrast between life and death, and their interrelation.

from: "An Interview With Robert Motherwell," Excerpt from *Artforum,* September 1965

The large format, at one blow, changed the century-long tendency of the French to domesticize modern painting, to make it intimate. We replaced the nude girl and the French door with a modern Stonehenge, with a sense of the sublime and the tragic that had not existed since Goya and Turner. What a gesture! Perhaps, someday, when we no longer threaten our contemporaries, someone will write our Iliad with empathy. One of the great images, like Achilles' shield, should be the housepainter's brush, in the employ of a grand vision dominated by an ethical sensibility that makes the usual painter's brush indeed picayune. How I admire my colleagues! So much so that I begrudge the coming new world nothing, not even its predominance of lovely young bodies.

Black on White. 1961. Oil on canvas, 78 x 162¾". The Museum of Fine Arts, Houston, Texas.

from: "A Major American Sculptor: David Smith" by Robert Motherwell, Excerpts from *Vogue*, February 1, 1965

I have known David Smith for twenty years, ever since that afternoon that we met by prearrangement (but unknown to each other) during the 1940s. We instinctively tried to drink each other under the table on Irish whiskey and Guinness Stout. We left each other late at night, wobbly, but walking. In those days I was full of French Symbolist aesthetics, of Rimbaud and Mallarmé, and of André Breton, of the possibilities of representing reality indirectly but passionately in one's medium. I can still see David saying, with his characteristic bluntness and inalterable sense of his own identity, "I don't know about those guys, I don't read French, but I don't need them. I've read James Joyce!" He was right, all of it *is* in *Ulysses,* and I looked at him with a sudden intellectual respect that has not diminished as my affection for him has continually grown.

When you see his burly figure in workman's clothes, you sense a cultivated man who knows his ancient and modern art intimately, including all the most recent developments. When you see him in Irish tweeds and with Monte Cristo cigars these past years, you are aware still of a man who spends most of his days cutting and welding hunks of steel often far too heavy for a single man to lift, driving his professional helpers as hard as himself, knowing that the workings of the greatest national economy the world has ever known are inadequate, not only to absorb his prodigious amount of work, but even to exhibit much of it.

It is not an especially comfortable place [Bolton Landing, New York], especially for women, but on its grounds, like sentinels, stands the greatest permanent one-man show of heroic contemporary sculpture in the Americas. A folk song runs: "It takes a worried man to sing a worried song." Well, it takes an iron will to have made all those weighty iron sculptures strewn about his mountain landscape, each silhouetted against an enormous sky.

For some years now during daylight hours, David Smith works on four separate streams of sculptural concepts simultaneously—painted pieces in which colour is of major importance, stainless steel structures, a series of iron "wagons" with bronze wheels, and heavy, welded structures of raw iron. At night, he continues an endless series of drawings ("the delicate pursuit of my life"). These are often nudes from life.

Oh David! You are as delicate as Vivaldi, and as strong as a Mack truck.

The French Line. (1960). Collage, 30 x 23". Collection Mr. and Mrs. Sam Hunter, New York.

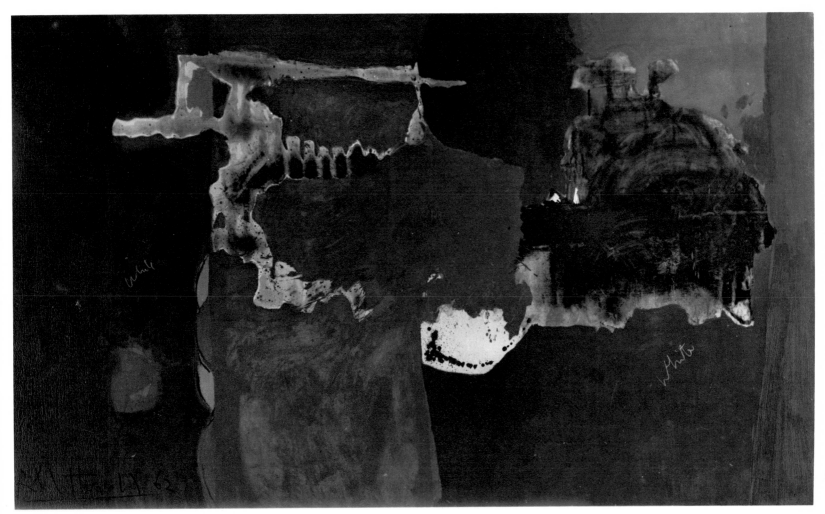

Chi Ama, Crede. 1962. Oil on canvas, 84 x 141". Collection the artist, courtesy of Marlborough-Gerson Gallery, New York.

Dear Frank:

While I think of it, would you amend (wherever it appears) the account of the school and The Club as follows: "The Friday Nights at the school led to the Friday Nights at The Club, the celebrated avant-garde artists club of the '50s, but other aspects of The Club grew out of another set of friendships at the old Waldorf cafeteria in the Village."

"I told a group of philosophers to their faces: Philosophy is simply a question of form!" Valéry, *Idée Fixe*, p. 107 (1932). I quote this half-appreciatively, half-ironically.

Intelligence often manifests itself in an excellent use of language. But laymen tend not to recognize that painting is also a language. (Indeed, what makes a layman is insensitivity to a given language.) In the case of painting, this surprisingly includes many people—certain painters, curators, critics, scholars, dealers—who are "professionals." No wonder the art scene is so often confusion.

But if intelligence is essential in order to organize relations, i.e., to arrive at structural form, then the subject-matter is feeling: art is not a science. Painting that does not radiate feeling is not worth looking at. The deepest—and rarest—of grown-up pleasures is true feeling.

When one is asked what painters one admires, one realizes one likes all the great ones. Who are more significant are those who invariably excite one to paint oneself: in my case, Rembrandt's drawings, Goya, Matisse and Picasso. On the other hand, the great van Eyck or Titian never incite me to work. Another test is those of one's contemporaries whose shows one looks forward to. These are few, but crucial. For me that has meant mostly Miró and a dozen Americans—and the possibility of anyone else anywhere.

It is a considerable achievement to have made one masterpiece in a lifetime.

An exhibition can never realize all one's desires from the world, even the most select and complete shows. Indeed, one feels how coarse and uncomprehending the world can be. But the real trauma is one's own reaction to one's work. As a great contemporary painter says: "If, after long contemplation, one feels one's life wasn't wasted, one has come out rather well."

Only painters and sculptors among artists can be exposed *in toto* in a few minutes—or seem to be.

The content has always to be expressed in modern terms: that is the basic premise. Joyce understood that perfectly.

The greater the precision of feeling, the more personal the work will be.

The more anonymous a work, the less universal, because in some paradoxical way, we understand the universal through the personal.

The dangers of recognition!

The problems of inventing a new language are staggering. But what else can one do if one needs to express one's feeling precisely?

It is the effort to respect one's feelings, one's integrity that leads to radical notions. No revolutionary was ever one for the hell of it: it is too painful a condition. But the pain is eased by its inevitability, given a real problem.

"One can never be as radical as reality itself." Lenin.

What paintings can stand up against the physical presence of nature? Few, and often least of all those who have nature as the principal subject.

Confusion always has the same cause: lack of genuine feeling.

Every picture one paints involves *not* painting others! What a choice!

Caution is the enemy of art, and everyone is more cautious than he thinks he is.

The drama of creativity is that one's resources, no matter how unusual, are inadequate.

The ultimate act is faith, the ultimate resource the preconscious: if either is suspended, the artist is impotent. This is possible any hour any day, and it is the artist's nightmare throughout life.

The fascination of sports figures, who must perform at a given place and time: but these are games.

What better way to spend one's life than to have, as one's primary task, the insistence on integrity of feeling? No wonder others are fascinated by artists.

We rush towards death.

Moments of joy make existence bearable: who ignores joy is immoral.

One longs to be treated by the grown-up world as one is by small children: with total trust.

One never really gets used to reality. The ultimate joke is our life of anxiety. God's small compensation is a sense of wonder.

But a sense of wonder can become a mannerism. No one is naive about everything, especially the talented.

The material things of life are mere decorations. Enough space, light, and white walls make any environment workable. Enough space and light, but not necessarily white, for that matter floods pictures with feeling.

The world cannot endure that artists' money comes from so much pleasure. Artists cannot endure that the world's money comes from so much work, and usually give extravagant tips and presents, as though our money were less "real."

I much prefer trading to selling, but not everyone who has something I need is an art-lover.

The surrealist group used to demand a picture each year from its painters: the proceeds were used to support their poets. They recognized the social injustice in the fact that a great painting has more commodity value than a great poem and equalized the situation. No one objected.

Contemporary paintings would not have to sell for so much if living artists received royalties from exhibitions and reproductions.

When artists are blamed for the financial madness of the art-scene, the psychology of collectors is left out of account.

Any picture is fairly priced, if its subsequent value is greater. And the years when one made nothing.

Recognition from The Establishment is only valuable in dealing with one's relatives, and one feels a parallel ambivalence: it is at once real and empty.

When I see a newsreel from 1915, the year I was born, or a movie that takes place then, like Jeanne Moreau's "Mata Hari," I cannot believe that my life span has been from that moment until the present: I had the same perspectives throughout, while the appearance of the world changed. When I was born is another universe, and I am 50. As though one were born in what is now a museum.

Whenever I hear talk about homosexuals, I remember that Proust's book is the greatest epic poem of the century. (Along with Joyce's *Ulysses*.)

The present vitality of American art is connected with the unparalleled depth of our democracy: it certainly did not come from cultural tradition, but from an existential context of greatly liberating forces.

New York City is a Constantinople, a great Bazaar. London is inexhaustible.

Parisian art was greatest when it was the most democratic and international city in Europe—1870-1939.

To modify one's art is to modify one's character. An artist whose work develops represents character growth, either slow and steady, like a garden, or in leaps, like Columbus' discovery of America.

The problem is to seize the glimpse.

The ethic lies in not making the glimpse presentable.

I could strangle those conservators who put glossy varnish on my pictures: what insensitivity to how their surfaces should feel.

If one paints on an enormous scale, one gets involved in all the problems of running a lumberyard. *(continued on page 67)*

Africa. 1964-65. Acrylic on canvas, 81 x 222½". The Baltimore Museum of Art, Baltimore, Maryland, gift of the artist.

top left: *Interior with Nude.* (1952). Oil on board, 9 x 12". Collection Mrs. Eleanor Ward, New York.

bottom left: *Iberia No. 18.* (1958). Oil on canvas, 5⅛ x 7⅛". Collection the artist.

top center: *Madrid No. 1.* (1958). Crayon and ink on paper, 15¼ x 24¼". Collection Professor and Mrs. Robert Gutman, Princeton, New Jersey.

bottom center: *Madrid No. 6.* (1958). Crayon and ink on paper, 15¾ x 17½". Collection the artist.

above: *A Spanish Elegy.* (1958). Oil on paper, 11½ x 14½". Coll. Mr. and Mrs. Bernard J. Reis, New York.

Jour la Maison, Nuit la Rue. (1957). Oil on canvas, 69¾ x 89⅝". Collection Mr. and Mrs. William C. Janss, Palm Desert, California.

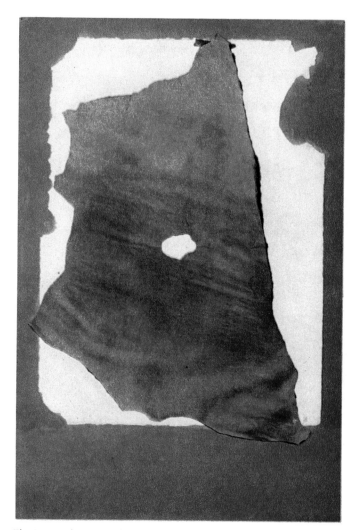

The Magic Skin (Peau de Chagrin). 1963. Oil and collage on cardboard, 39¾ x 26⅞". Yale University Art Gallery, New Haven, Connecticut, gift of the artist.

N.R.F. Collage #1. 1959. Oil and collage, sight: 28½ x 22½". Whitney Museum of American Art, New York, gift of the Friends of the Whitney Museum.

N.R.F. Collage #2. 1960. Collage, sight: 28⅜ x 21½". Whitney Museum of American Art, New York, gift of the Friends of the Whitney Museum.

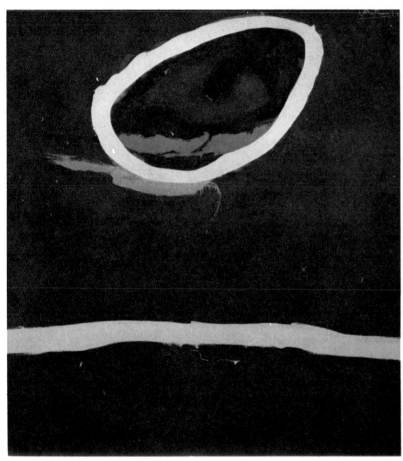

Indian Summer, #1. 1962-64. Oil and acrylic on canvas, 70⅛ x 63". Collection Kenneth Noland, South Shaftsbury, Vermont.

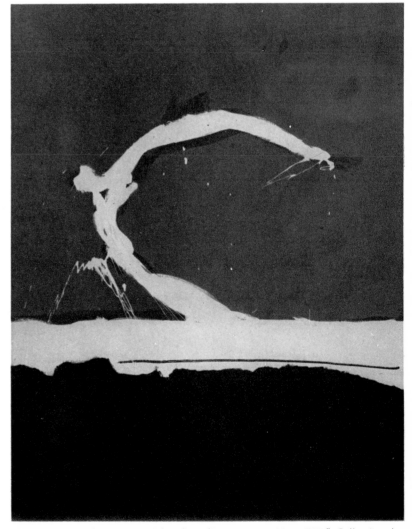

Indian Summer, #2. 1962-64. Oil and acrylic on canvas, 66⅛ x 50⅛". Collection the artist, courtesy of Marlborough-Gerson Gallery, New York.

66

Elegy to the Spanish Republic LVII. 1957-60. Oil on canvas, 84 x 108⅞". Collection Mr. and Mrs. Gardner Hempel, Littleton, Colorado.

Irony, the greatest necessity of everyday life, does not work in pictures. (Neither does pathos.)

If one has capital, and no respect for it *per se,* one can accomplish miraculous projects. Contrary to rumor, I never did have it.

Little pictures are for midgets or for tourists—souvenirs.

This summer in Europe . . . .

What secrets are hidden in Venice!

How everybody in the Aegean slaughtered everybody! No wonder all is ruins!

Chi ama, crede: who loves, trusts.

The miracle of a good marriage is that one's qualities are enhanced and strengthened into a continuity that no one can sustain alone.

I am astonished at all the very young artists now who do not seem to reflect—as my generation did—on how expensive children are. None of us had children before 40, and most not at all.

As David Smith liked to say, "To be an artist is a luxury."

Alex Liberman likes to say, "Nothing is too good for artists."

There is something princely about even the most democratic artists.

Art is much less important than life, but what a poor life without it! This is not aestheticism, but recognition that art as much as anything—perhaps more—conveys how men feel to themselves. In this sense, even the most difficult art is meant to be shared, and does communicate.

One does not have to "understand" wholly to feel pleasure.

One can't think clearly without thinking in alternatives. Blankness is the failure of an alternative to come to mind.

It's a good thing that there is not an after-life. What would one do with it through eternity? There's not that much capacity in the human substance.

If life were longer, one could express more. Since it isn't, stick to essentials.

Every artist needs a model. Not to paint, but as a beautiful living presence. Art that has no element of the erotic is like a life without the erotic, shrivelled.

Modern European culture castrated itself when it killed the Jews.

The power in saying no!

It's not the art in Greece that ravishes everyone: other civilizations have greater monuments—it's the pervasive nakedness!

What has the world got to tempt an artist? What is more desirable than feeling?

To feel like a man. What is better?

A man of feeling has a right to be furious.

I would fight more if I had more time.

We are saved from the word: There is more than one *can* read!

The beauty of another being's presence.

It's better to be brutal than indifferent.

An artist *cares.* That is what can be trusted.

Some children quit painting if they haven't the proper color. Picasso says, you just use another color. Who's right?

Drawing is dividing the surface plane.

Color is a question of quantity, i.e., extension in space.

But it is light that counts above everything. Not colored light, but color that gives off light—radiance!

The supreme gift, after light, is scale.

The technique of painting is the simplest of all the arts: For that reason it demands the greatest sensibility.

I love poetry and music, but I would rather see.

Somebody ought to invent an inflatable studio. Then painters would be free to travel. (The predicament of sculptors is hopeless.)

Throw of Dice, #17. 1963. Oil on canvas, 72⅛ x 48⅛". Collection Mr. and Mrs. Robert H. Shoenberg, St. Louis, Missouri.

The beauty of Europe is that sculpture is everywhere. The sculpture doesn't have to be great to function perfectly in the landscape, humanizing it.

America is what the poor people of Europe invented, given means enough and time. Europeans therefore shouldn't snub it.

The miracle of a place that one likes to go *home* to, prefers to any other. Which means to *someone*.

Homer, Shakespeare, Mozart and *l'art moderne* fill my pantheon: the rest is extra.

The only thing that I bought in Greece (1965) was a scale-model of a Homeric ship.

The adequate application of psycho-analysis to an artist is George Painter's two-volume *Marcel Proust*. The subject is ideal and the application a marvel of precision and completeness.

The world is more indebted than it seems to know to Francoise Gilot's *Life With Picasso*. It, perhaps more than any other book, should be required reading for every aspiring modern artist.

David Smith many years ago saw Ernst Kris [author of *Psycho-analytic Explorations in Art*] twice—who was already dying, and who apparently told David to endure it all, to live with it. But in the end he couldn't. Oh, David!

Every painter *au fond* is a voyeur: the question is whether he has a vision.

Painting is a totally active act.

From my writings, it would seem that I am more interested in poetry than painting, which of course is not at all true. It is that the poets have speculated much more in words about what "the modern" is. When I used to defend "modern art" during the early struggles of abstract expressionism, I often turned to the poets for suggestions and arguments against the Philistines.

My writing does not compare, in depth or originality, with my painting. But most people are more at home with writing.

Summertime in Italy #7—In Golden Ochre. 1961. Oil on canvas, 85 x 69⅛". Collection the artist, courtesy of Marlborough-Gerson Gallery, New York.

Summertime in Italy #8. 1960. Oil on canvas, 100⅜ x 70⅜". Collection the artist, courtesy of the Marlborough-Gerson Gallery, New York.

Having a retrospective is making a will.

What better definition of modern art is there than Mallarmé's "... the expression of the mysterious meaning of aspects of existence, through human language brought back to its essential rhythm: in this way, it endows our sojourn with authenticity, and constitutes the only spiritual task," or (1864): "... for I am inventing a language that must necessarily spring from a very new poetics: *to paint, not the thing, but the effect that it produces.*"

What I have never had a chance to write about (though I have sometimes lectured on it) is the changes that were brought about by the transplanting of the modern aesthetic into America: that is the real story of abstract expressionism. And part of its story is its extension of "the modern" during a decade (1940s) when European belief in the modern greatly weakened: we here had already been through those alternatives in the 30s and had rejected them.

The interest in language so dominant in modern art is not an interest in semantics *per se:* it is a continual interest in making language (whatever the medium) to fit our real feelings better, and even to be able to express true feelings that had never been capable of expression before. How much more humanistic in the end is this effort on the part of solitary individuals than that of those who throw a collective ideology at one and say, that is the obvious truth, now express it! It is only authoritarian groups, whether political or religious, who can determine by pressure the *future* of their arts. To us who are freer individually, the future is a wide-open adventure of unimagined possibilities, and of hundreds of booby-traps.

I regret that I have referred to the French so much in my life, because it gives the impression of something a bit precious and over-cultivated. Actually, I hardly could be more American in most of my aspects, and I speak French as an oriental house-boy speaks English. Nor am I especially interested in France. My interest is in certain ideas about *modern art*. The French developed them in painting and poetry for a long time, but the man who has the strongest claim to be the father of the concept of the modern as we know it is an American, Edgar Allan Poe; and in painting at least, America has developed ideas about modern art more rigorously than any country since World War II. The other great tradition of these past 200 years has been the English and Russian novel, followed by the movies, which I enjoyed as much as anyone, but which by-and-large has little to do with painting—with modern painting, at least, which is symbolic and poetic, not discursive and descriptive. But the latter is always trying to infiltrate modern painting, usually under the tag of some "humanism" or another. What shit!

For me the extraordinary English artists of the 19th century are Dickens, Turner, and Hopkins; in America, Poe, Melville, Whitman, Ryder and Eakins. But one has to wait until the 20th century to talk about modern art in clusters: in this sense, in our century the enterprise is more sociable, less desperate.

I love Hopkins' insistence on particularization.

Barnett Newman for years has said that when he reads my writings, he learns what I have been reading, but when he wants to know what I am really concerned with at a given moment, he looks at my pictures. He's right.

To have the discipline to shut-up, and just paint the pictures!

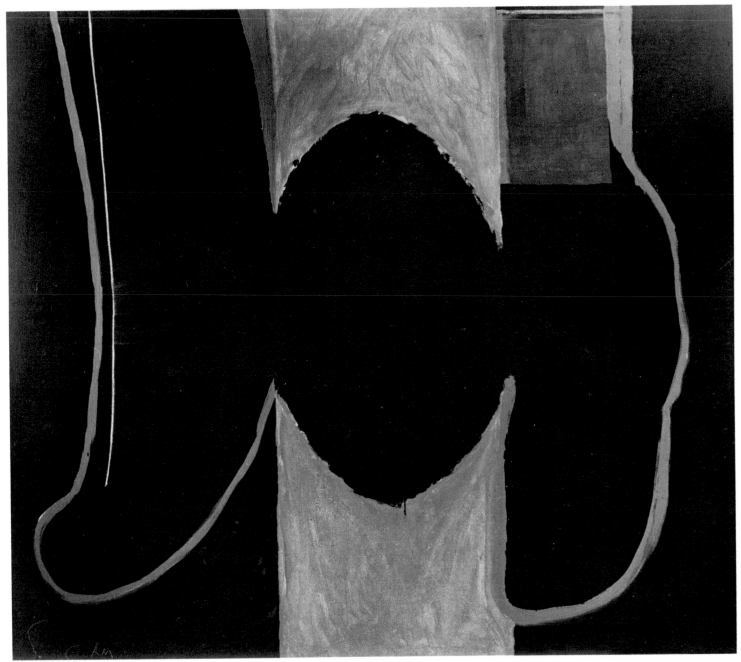

Irish Elegy. 1965. Acrylic on canvas, 69⅜ x 83¾″. Collection the artist, courtesy of Marlborough-Gerson Gallery, New York.

1915
Born in Aberdeen, Washington, on January 24, to Robert Burns Motherwell II and Margaret Motherwell (née Hogan). Father has job in local bank; mother is daughter of local lawyer and intellectual. (The great-grandmother Hogan, whom he knew, left Ireland in the great famine of 1846. The Scots Motherwell grandfather left Scotland in the mid-nineteenth century as the youngest of eleven brothers, who were "land poor").

1916
Sister Mary-Stuart born on August 24 (now Mrs. William Bosschart, Hillsborough, California).

1918
Family moves to San Francisco, California. The father, twenty years later, becomes a successful banker. Lives in San Francisco until 1937, except for five years in the 1920s in Salt Lake City, Utah and Los Angeles, California.

1926
Receives fellowship to the Otis Art Institute in Los Angeles when eleven. (Because too young, not allowed in life classes, so paints from imagination: knights, armor, shields, battleflags, medieval heraldry.) Most summers after 1926 spent at seashore near Aberdeen, Washington which gave the artist a life-long bias for living near the sea. Meets there his first artist, Lance Hart, who encourages him.

1929
Because of developing asthma, attends Moran Preparatory School in Atascadero, California, until 1932, when he graduates.

1932
Studies painting briefly at the California School of Fine Arts in San Francisco. Spends the summer as usual near Aberdeen, Washington.

Motherwell in his studio, 1943. To the left *Collage in Beige and Black*, 1944 (page 20) and on the right the unfinished *Wall Painting with Stripes*, 1944 (page 24).

Motherwell at the age of 15.

Enters Stanford University, Stanford, California. During his stay at Stanford is deeply impressed by seeing the Matisse collection of the Michael Steins (brother and sister-in-law of Gertrude and Leo Stein).

He finds the art department of Stanford uninteresting and finally majors in philosophy. During his last years at the University he rooms with Henry David Aiken, who ultimately becomes Professor of Philosophy at Harvard University. Through Aiken becomes interested in music, especially Bach, Haydn, and Mozart. Hears Igor Stravinsky play and Gertrude Stein lecture at Stanford.

Writes undergraduate thesis on O'Neill's relation to psychoanalytic theory (the latter becomes a life-long interest).

1935
First visit to Europe: tours France, Italy, Switzerland, Germany, Holland, Belgium, England and Scotland (including Motherwell, near Glasgow) with father and sister during summer.

Beginning of studies in French literature, from Baudelaire to the *Nouvelle Revue Française*. Writes on André Gide. Reads Proust.

1936
Receives A.B. degree in philosophy from Stanford University.

1937
Hears André Malraux speak on the Spanish Civil War at a rally in San Francisco.

To Cambridge, Massachusetts to enter Graduate School of Arts and Sciences of Harvard University, enrolling in the department of Philosophy. Studies aesthetics under Professors Arthur O. Lovejoy and David W. Prall, but affected by Alfred North Whitehead's presence and studies his writings. Writes thesis on Delacroix's journals, and is advised by Lovejoy and Prall to do further research in Paris.

1938
Spends the summer at the University of Grenoble, France after a year at Harvard.

Visits Delacroix exhibition in Zurich.

1939
Visits England; spends a short time at Oxford University. Translates Paul Signac's *D'Eugène Delacroix au Néo-Impressionisme* (manuscript lost on a ship during World War II).

Returns to U.S.A. in August.

Appointed assistant in art at the University of Oregon, Eugene, Oregon.

1940
After year at University of Oregon spends last summer in Aberdeen. In September sails through Panama Canal for New York City, where he has lived ever since (except for several years on Long Island).

Enters Department of Art History and Archaeology of Columbia University, New York City. As a graduate student he studies under Professor Meyer Schapiro (recommended to him by Arthur Berger, the composer). Schapiro introduces him to some of the surrealist artists living in exile in New York City and encourages him to devote himself to the act of painting rather than to scholarship.

Impressed by an abstract steel "Head" by a young American sculptor, David Smith, in an outdoor exhibition in Greenwich Village.

1941

Studies engraving for a short time with Kurt Seligmann. Becomes friendly with the surrealist artists in exile. The international surrealist group in and around New York includes Matta Echaurren, with whom he becomes especially friendly, Marcel Duchamp, Max Ernst, Esteban Francés, Stanley William Hayter, Wifredo Lam, André Masson, Gordon Onslow-Ford, Kurt Seligmann, Yves Tanguy, and the poet André Breton. Remains closely associated with them for four years (although his own painting is always considered too "abstract" by them).

Meets other artists in exile including Marc Chagall, Frederick Kiesler, Fernand Léger, Jacques Lipchitz, Piet Mondrian, Amédée Ozenfant, and Ossip Zadkine, as well as Alexander Calder and Isamu Noguchi. Encounters the work of Joseph Cornell through Matta.

Becomes deeply interested in surrealist theories, particularly "automatism," in accordance with his interest in Freudian psychoanalysis and the poetics of the French Symbolists, but his main interest is in the more abstract artists, particularly Hans Arp, Paul Klee, Henri Matisse, Joan Miró, Piet Mondrian, and Pablo Picasso.

Decides to devote himself professionally to painting.

During the summer visits Mexico with Matta. Stays on through the fall to work with Wolfgang Paalen.

Marries a Mexican actress, Maria Emilia Ferreira y Moyers.

Returns to New York City.

Paints *Little Spanish Prison*.

1942

Because of asthmatic history found unfit for military service.

Meets William Baziotes and through him Jackson Pollock, and through Pollock, Hans Hofmann and Willem de Kooning.

In the original prospectus for the magazine *VVV*, devoted to "imaginative works of universal interest, whether they be in poetry, the plastic arts, anthropology, psychology, sociology, the evolution of science, comparative religion, or in what may simply be called the field of the wonderful," announced as the editor, with Breton, William Carlos Williams, Ernst, and Matta as editorial advisers, as well as many of the outstanding figures in art and literature who were particularly interested in surrealism at the time. Resigns, to be replaced by Lionel Abel, who resigns later. Only three issues appeared, all actually edited by David Hare. In the first issue, Motherwell writes on Mondrian and Giorgio de Chirico. He is also among those (in the first issue) who classify their attractions to various creatures in mythology and legend. Of the fifteen creatures he lists his favorite as being the Unicorn, and the least-liked Narcissus.

Sees Mondrian's first one-man show at Valentine Dudensing's gallery in New York City.

Gives a picture to Pollock.

Makes "automatic" poems with the Baziotes and the Pollocks.

Visits often the A. E. Gallatin Collection of avant-garde art at New York University (now in the Philadelphia Museum of Art).

Many meetings with Matta, and also with the composer, John Cage.

Included in "First Papers of Surrealism," an exhibition organized by André Breton and Marcel Duchamp for the Coordinating Council of French Relief Societies Inc. and held in the vacant Whitelaw Reid Mansion, 451 Madison Avenue, New York City.

1943

Peggy Guggenheim invites Baziotes, Motherwell, and Pollock to submit collages to a forthcoming collage exhibition at her gallery. Motherwell and Pollock make their first collages together in Pollock's studio. Collage becomes a major interest for Motherwell.

Paints his first nearly totally black pictures.

Visits Mexico.

Father dies of cancer in San Francisco.

Motherwell returns to New York City.

1944

Becomes director of "The Documents of Modern Art," a series of illustrated publications on contemporary art, published by George Wittenborn and Heinz Schultz, New York. Bernard Karpel, Librarian, The Museum of Modern Art, New York, makes the bibliographies for the entire series and many crucial suggestions. Writes preface for Guillaume Apollinaire's *The Cubist Painters*, the first of the series to appear. (Revised preface for later edition.)

Writes art chronicle for *Partisan Review* on Mondrian and The Museum of Modern Art's acquisition of that artist's *Broadway Boogie Woogie*, an Alexander Calder retrospective at The Museum of Modern Art, and Jackson Pollock's first one-man exhibition at Art of This Century Gallery.

Lectures on "The Modern Painter's World" as guest of "Pontigny-en-Amérique," Jean Wahl, Chairman, at Mt. Holyoke College, South Hadley, Massachusetts. (Subsequently printed in *Dyn*, November, 1944).

Summer in East Hampton, Long Island.

First museum purchase: *Pancho Villa, Dead and Alive*, 1943, by The Museum of Modern Art, New York.

First one-man exhibition, at Peggy Guggenheim's Art of This Century Gallery in New York City. It includes three important collages, *Joy of Living* (Baltimore Museum, Saidie A. May Collection), *Surprise and Inspiration* (Peggy Guggenheim Collection, Venice), and *Pancho Villa, Dead and Alive*.

1945

Studies engraving for about a month with Stanley William Hayter.

Offered contract by Samuel M. Kootz, as are Baziotes, Adolph Gottlieb, and Hofmann.

During the spring Motherwell and Baziotes travel to Florida because of their interest in its "southern light."

Becomes friendly with Gottlieb.

Motherwell at his first one-man show in Peggy Guggenheim's "Art of This Century" gallery in 1944.

Max Ernst and Motherwell playing chess, Amagansett, Long Island, 1944.

Teaching at Black Mountain College, North Carolina, 1950.

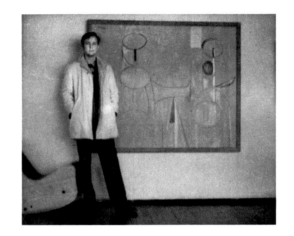

"Artists in Exile" as shown by Pierre Matisse Gallery. First row from left to right: Matta Echaurren, Ossip Zadkine, Yves Tanguy, Max Ernst, Marc Chagall, Fernand Léger. Second row from left to right: André Breton, Piet Mondrian, André Masson, Amédée Ozenfant, Jacques Lipchitz, Pavel Tchelitchew, Kurt Seligmann, Eugene Berman. Photograph by George Platt Lynes.

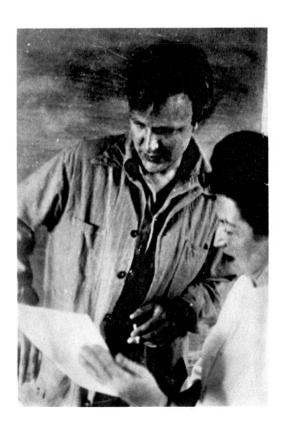

THE SUBJECTS OF THE ARTIST:

a new art school
35 East 8th Street, New York 3, New York.

Catalogue for 1948-49

ARTISTS: William Baziotes, David Hare, Robert Motherwell, Mark Rothko.

THEORY OF THE SCHOOL: The artists who have formed this school believe that receiving instruction in regularly scheduled courses from a single teacher is not necessarily the best spirit in which to advance creative work. Those who are in a learning stage benefit most by associating with working artists and developing with them variations on the artistic process (through actually drawing, painting, and sculpting). If the 'student' so prefers, he can choose one artist on the faculty and work exclusively with him. But it is the school's belief that more is to be gained by exposure to the different subjects of all four artists—to what modern artists paint about, as well as how they paint. It will be possible to work with a single artist only in evening sessions, since the afternoon sessions are the responsibility of the faculty as a whole.

CURRICULUM: There are no formal courses. Each afternoon and evening session will be conducted by one of the four artists as a spontaneous investigation into the subjects of the modern artist—what his subjects are, how they are arrived at, methods of inspiration and transformation, moral attitudes, possibilities for further explorations, what is being done now and what might be done, and so on. The afternoon sessions are from 1:30 to 4:30, and the evening sessions from 7:30 to 10:30. There is no instruction on Fridays, when the school will be at the disposal of the students for independent work. The school is closed on Saturdays, Sundays, and certain holidays.

STUDENTS: Those attending the classes will not be treated as 'students' in the conventional manner, but as collaborators with the artists in the investigation of the artistic process, its modern conditions, possibilities, and extreme nature, through discussions and practise.

REQUIREMENTS: There are no technical requirements; beginners and those who paint for themselves are welcome; the school is for anyone who wishes to reach beyond conventional modes of expression.

REGULATIONS: Smoking will be regulated according to the fire laws; anyone who does not fit in the school will be asked to withdraw (with refund of unused tuition).

TERMS: (each of ten weeks)
11 October - 17 December, 1948
3 January - 11 March, 1949
21 March - 27 May, 1949

FEES: (payable in advance by term or year)

	Term	Year
One evening a week	45.	125.
Two evenings a week	80.	225.
Four evenings a week	150.	400.
Five afternoons a week	150.	400.

In regard to any further particulars, please write or telephone the Secretary of the school.

Announcement for School, The Subjects of the Artist, 1948-49.

Elegy to the Spanish Republic I. (1948). Ink on paper, sight: 10½ x 8⅛". Collection the artist. Decoration for a poem by Harold Rosenberg.

Commissioned by Curtice Hitchcock to illustrate Marianne Moore's translation of La Fontaine's *Fables*. (Later canceled on death of publisher.)

Writes preface for Mondrian's *Plastic Art and Pure Plastic Art,* the second of the "Documents of Modern Art" series.

Teaches during the summer at Black Mountain College, Black Mountain, North Carolina.

1946

Wassily Kandinsky's *Concerning the Spiritual in Art* and *The New Vision* by László Moholy-Nagy are published as the third and fourth of the "Documents of Modern Art" series.

Becomes friendly with Barnett Newman, Mark Rothko, and Herbert Ferber.

Summer in East Hampton; lives there until the fall of 1948.

Exhibition at Kootz Gallery, New York City.

Exhibition at the San Francisco Museum of Art, California.

Exhibition at the Arts Club of Chicago, Illinois.

Included in "Fourteen Americans" at The Museum of Modern Art, New York.

1947

Builds house and studio in East Hampton, designed for him by the late Pierre Chareau. The design was adapted from the Quonset huts of World War II. (Chareau was a noted French designer, and in his youth a collector of Cubist works, who designed the Free French Canteen in New York City, a center for the artists in exile). House and studio, later sold to Barney Rossett, cause great financial strain.

Louis Sullivan's *Kindergarten Chats* is published as the fifth of the "Documents of Modern Art" series.

Exhibition at Kootz Gallery, New York City.

Included in exhibition of "Three Americans," with Baziotes and Gottlieb, at the Galerie Maeght in Paris.

1948

Paints *The Homely Protestant,* a relatively figurative abstraction, the title of which actually came from Motherwell's placing his finger at random on a page of James Joyce's *Finnegans Wake.*

Robert Motherwell School of Fine Art Painting Drawing Theory 61 Fourth Ave., N. Y. C. Tues., Wed., 7-10 P. M.

Announcement for Robert Motherwell School of Fine Art, 1948-49.

Clyfford Still that summer proposes a cooperative art school which is agreed to by Baziotes, David Hare, Motherwell, and Rothko. A cold-water loft is rented at 35 East 8th Street, New York City, and Bernard J. Reis donates the heating system. The School is called "The Subjects of the Artist" (to emphasize that abstract painting has a subject matter). Still withdraws before its opening; at mid-year Barnett Newman joins the faculty. On Friday evenings other artists are invited to speak to the students and out of this grows the Friday evenings of Studio 35 and "The Club," where the avant-garde artists and writers meet weekly for discussion during the 50's; but other aspects of "The Club" grow out of another set of friendships formed by artists meeting at the nearby Waldorf Cafeteria (now torn down). The School closes permanently at the end of the spring term in 1949.

Edits *Possibilities (An Occasional Review)* with John Cage, Pierre Chareau and Harold Rosenberg (published by Wittenborn and Schultz). Only one issue appeared.

Begins what is later known as the "Elegy to the Spanish Republic" series. Discovers motif when decorating a page of a poem by Harold Rosenberg for reproduction in projected second issue of *Possibilities*.

Becomes friendly with Bradley Walker Tomlin, who is introduced by Gottlieb.

Writes prefatory notes for Hans Arp's *On My Way*, the sixth of the "Documents of Modern Art" series, and for Max Ernst's *Beyond Painting*, the seventh.

Exchanges pictures with Rothko.

Exhibition at Kootz Gallery, New York City.

The "Irascibles." Seated from left to right: Theodoros Stamos, Jimmy Ernst, Jackson Pollock, Barnett Newman, James Brooks, Mark Rothko. Standing from left to right: Richard Pousette-Dart, William Baziotes, Willem de Kooning, Adolph Gottlieb, Ad Reinhardt, Hedda Sterne, Clyfford Still, Robert Motherwell, Bradley Walker Tomlin. Photograph by Nina Leen, courtesy LIFE Magazine © 1951 Time, Inc.

1949

Paints *The Voyage* (now owned by The Museum of Modern Art, New York) and *Granada*, the first large Spanish Elegy (now in the Nelson A. Rockefeller Collection) in uninterrupted eighteen-hour periods during two blizzards in December 1948 and January 1949. Motherwell is later persuaded by Tomlin not to destroy them.

After demise of "The Subjects of the Artist" school he starts his own Robert Motherwell School of Fine Art (painting, drawing, theory) on Fourth Avenue, near 10th Street, New York City, in the fall, which lasts one year.

Shares his school-studio with Tomlin for this year.

Writes preliminary notice for Daniel-Henry Kahnweiler's *The Rise of Cubism*, the eighth of the "Documents of Modern Art" series and for Marcel Raymond's *From Baudelaire to Surrealism*, the ninth.

Exhibition of collages (1943-1949) at Kootz Gallery, New York City. (Note by the poet Marianne Moore included in exhibition pamphlet.)

Included in "The Intrasubjectives" at Kootz Gallery with Arshile Gorky, Ad Reinhardt, de Kooning, Pollock, Rothko and Tomlin.

1950

Paints sketch for mural for The Architects' Collaborative (Walter Gropius, etc.) project in Attleboro, Massachusetts; project never realized.

Paints *Mural Fragment* later acquired by the University Gallery, the University of Minnesota, Minneapolis, Minnesota.

Joins the so-called "Irascibles" including Baziotes, de Kooning, Gottlieb, Hofmann, Newman, Pollock, Richard Pousette-Dart, Reinhardt, Rothko, Still and Tomlin in writing an open letter to Roland L. Redmond, President of The Metropolitan Museum of Art, protesting against hostility toward the avant-garde in the organization of a large exhibition of American art.

Writes catalogue preface at David Smith's request. Meets him for the first time in conjunction with it.

Marries Betty Little of Washington, D. C.

Georges Duthuit's *The Fauvist Painters* is published as the tenth of the "Documents of Modern Art" series.

Exhibition of Elegies, Capriccios, Wall Paintings, and drawings (Nudes, Spanish Elegies, Cocks and Capriccios) at Kootz Gallery, New York City.

Granada included in "Black or White: Paintings by European and American Artists" at Kootz Gallery. Writes preface for catalogue. Meets Franz Kline who is deeply affected by *Granada*.

Included in *The Muralist and the Modern Architect* at Kootz Gallery. The other muralists are Baziotes, Gottlieb, and Hans Hofmann.

1951

Edits *The Dada Painters and Poets: An Anthology*, the eleventh of the "Documents of Modern Art" series, the major publication on this movement, and writes a preface and an introduction. At the time this book influences poets more than painters.

Paints mural for the synagogue of Congregation B'nai Israel in Millburn, New Jersey. Other artists collaborating are Herbert Ferber, Adolph Gottlieb, and architect Percival Goodman.

Participates in a panel "What Abstract Art Means to Me" held at The Museum of Modern Art, New York. Others participating are: Alexander Calder, Stuart Davis, de Kooning, Fritz Glarner, and George L. K. Morris. Statements later published by The Museum of Modern Art.

Lectures on "The Rise and Continuity of Abstract Art" at the Fogg Art Museum, Cambridge, Massachusetts, with Oliver Larkin, Meyer Schapiro, and Ben Shahn.

Lectures on "The Poetry of Abstract Painting" at the Philadelphia Museum of Art.

Appointed Associate Professor at Hunter College of the City University of New York, and during next seven years helps Professor Edna Wells Luetz reorganize the art department.

Becomes friendly with Philip Guston.

Teaches during the summer at Black Mountain College. Among the students there are Fielding Dawson, Francine de Plessix, Robert Rauschenberg, Dan Rice, and Cy Twombly.

Included in "The School of New York" at Frank Perls Gallery, Beverly Hills, California, for which he writes the preface to the catalogue. (This is the first use of the term "School of New York.")

Included in "Ninth Street," an exhibition of paintings and sculpture by artists working in that vicinity in New York City.

Included in "Forty American Painters, 1940-1950" at the University of Minnesota, Minneapolis, Minnesota.

Included in the U. S. Representation at the II Bienal in São Paulo, Brazil.

1952

Edits *Modern Artists in America* with Ad Reinhardt, and designs the book jacket. Bernard Karpel provides extensive documentation, and Aaron Siskind the photography. It chronicled important symposia on modern art held in New York and San Francisco and it remains one of the important documents of that time.

Gives graduate seminar at Oberlin College, Oberlin, Ohio. Exhibition of paintings and drawings at the Allen Memorial Art Museum of Oberlin College, at invitation of Charles Parkhurst.

Included in "American Vanguard Art for Paris" at the Galerie de France, Paris.

1953

Daughter Jeannie is born.

Buys old brownstone house on East 94th Street, where he still lives, after sale of East Hampton house.

Writes on Joseph Cornell.

Designs tapestry for Congregation Beth-El, Springfield, Massachusetts.

One of "Four Abstract Expressionists" shown at the Walker Art Center, Minneapolis, Minnesota. The other three are Baziotes, Gottlieb, and Hofmann.

Exhibition of paintings, drawings and collages at Kootz Gallery.

1954

Teaches during the summer at Colorado Springs Fine Arts Center, Colorado Springs, Colorado. Becomes friendly with Emerson Woelffer there, and they exchange pictures.

Fishes with Red Stripe. 1954. Oil on paper, 42½ x 41⅛".
Collection John Murray Cuddihy, New York.

Pink Nude with Bowed Head. 1958. Oil on paper
mounted on cardboard, 23⅞ x 19½". Collection Miss
Helen Frankenthaler, New York.

Motherwell with Barnett Newman at the Brussels
World's Fair, 1959.

Motherwell with Helen Frankenthaler in front of their
house in Provincetown, Massachusetts, summer, 1962.
Photograph by David Smith.

Poster for exhibition at Sidney Janis Gallery, 1959.

Guest of The Federal Republic of Germany under an exchange program together with a group of architects, industrial designers and educators. Richard Lippold is also invited, and the two become friendly.

Included in the U. S. Representation at the Tenth Inter-American Conference in Caracas, Venezuela. (Others represented are Baziotes, Gorky, Kline, Pollock, and Rothko).

Included in "Object and Image in Modern Art and Poetry" at the Yale University Art Gallery, New Haven, Connecticut.

Included in "Younger American Painters: A Selection" at the Solomon R. Guggenheim Museum, New York City.

1955

Daughter Lise is born.

Included in the U. S. Representation at the "Third International Art Exhibition," Japan, shown in eight cities there.

Included in "The New Decade: Thirty-five American Painters and Sculptors," at the Whitney Museum of American Art, New York City, shown subsequently in San Francisco, Los Angeles, Colorado Springs, and St. Louis.

Included in "Modern Art in the United States: Selections from the Collections of The Museum of Modern Art, New York." Shown 1955-56 in Paris, Zürich, Barcelona, Frankfurt, London, The Hague, Vienna, and Belgrade.

1956

Spends summer in Provincetown, Massachusetts and returns there often in other summers. Joins a perennial poker game.

Addresses Convocation of Trinity College, Hartford, Connecticut. He emphasizes the ethical aspect of art. Among those participating are Francis Henry Taylor, Lionel Trilling, and Richard Wilbur.

1957

Writes on Tomlin for catalogue of his memorial exhibition.

Exhibition of paintings and collages at Sidney Janis

Gallery, New York City. First sizable earnings from paintings slowly begin.

Buys eighteenth-century house in Provincetown.

Meets Helen Frankenthaler in late autumn.

Included in "American Paintings: 1945-1957" at The Minneapolis Institute of Arts, Minneapolis, Minnesota.

1958

Takes sabbatical from teaching post at Hunter College. Marries Helen Frankenthaler in the spring.

Spends summer in Spain and France, mainly at St. Jean-de-Luz.

Included in "The New American Painting," a major exhibition of Abstract Expressionism organized by The Museum of Modern Art, New York. Shown 1958-59 in Basel, Milan, Madrid, Berlin, Amsterdam, Brussels, Paris, London, and New York.

Included in "Seventeen Contemporary American Painters" in the exhibition of American Art at the Brussels Universal and International Exhibition.

Included in the "International Art Festival," Osaka, Japan.

1959

Invited to discuss a paper, "Modern Art and Human Development, A Psychoanalytic Comment," presented by Charles R. Hulbeck, M.D. (Richard Huelsenbeck) at the Association for the Advancement of Psychoanalysis, New York City.

Writes on Miró.

Resigns from Hunter College.

Summer in Provincetown. David Smith makes first of annual visits with his children.

First retrospective at Bennington College, Bennington, Vermont, at invitation of Eugene Goosen.

Exhibition of paintings, drawings, and collages at Sidney Janis Gallery, New York City.

Included in "American Painting and Sculpture," part of the American National Exhibition in Moscow.

Included in U. S. Representation at Documenta II, Kassel, Germany.

Included in "New York and Paris: Painting in the Fifties" at the Museum of Fine Arts, Houston, Texas.

1960

Interviewed for the British Broadcasting Corporation by David Sylvester. The broadcast was under Sylvester's title "Painting as Self-Discovery." A transcription appeared in *Metro* as "Painting as Existence," a title preferred by Motherwell.

Summer in Alassio, Italy.

Participates in panel at the Philadelphia Museum School of Art on "The Concept of the New." Others participating are Guston, Reinhardt, Harold Rosenberg, and Jack Tworkov as moderator.

Included in "Paths of Abstract Art" at the Cleveland Museum of Art, Cleveland, Ohio, and in "Contemporary American Painting" at the Columbus Gallery of Fine Arts, Columbus, Ohio.

Helen Frankenthaler Motherwell with the artist's daughters, Lise and Jeannie. Winter 1961-62.

Included in "Sixty American Painters 1960: Abstract Expressionist Painting of the Fifties" at the Walker Art Center, Minneapolis, Minnesota.

1961

Among the signers of a statement "In Support of the French Intellectuals" who were being victimized for their criticism of the Algerian war. The statement appeared in the United States in the January-February issue of *Partisan Review*.

Joins in a letter to the editor protesting as insulting the criticism of *New York Times* art critic, John Canaday. Among others signing are de Kooning, Gottlieb, Hofmann, Barnett Newman, David Smith, Thomas B. Hess, Sam Hunter, Harold Rosenberg, Irving H. Sandler, and Meyer Schapiro.

Visits London and Paris.

Summer in Provincetown.

Retrospective exhibition selected by Frank O'Hara for U. S. participation at VI Bienal in São Paulo, organized by The Museum of Modern Art, New York.

Exhibition of paintings and collages at Sidney Janis Gallery, New York City.

Exhibition of collages (1958-60) at Galerie Berggruen, Paris.

Included in "The Art of Assemblage" at The Museum of Modern Art, New York, shown thereafter in Dallas and San Francisco.

Included in "American Abstract Expressionists and Imagists" at the Solomon R. Guggenheim Museum, New York City.

Included in "Modern American Drawings," an exhibition organized by The Museum of Modern Art, New York. Shown in Spoleto, Jerusalem, Athens, Helsinki, Göteborg, Paris, London, and Bonn.

Included in *American Vanguard* organized by the United States Information Agency. Shown in Vienna and Belgrade.

1962

Appointed visiting critic at the University of Pennsylvania Graduate School of Fine Arts in Philadelphia. Other critics are Barnett Newman and David Smith

Exchanges pictures with Kenneth Noland.

Retrospective exhibition (based on that shown at VI Bienal, São Paulo) at the Pasadena Art Museum, Pasadena, California, at the invitation of Thomas W. Leavitt; also delivers a lecture there on the occasion.

Exhibition of paintings and collages at Sidney Janis Gallery, New York City. "Beside the Sea" series shown publicly for the first time.

Exhibition of collages (1958-1960) at the Galleria Odyssia, Rome and at the Galerie der Spiegel, Cologne, Germany.

Included in "Art since 1950" at the Seattle World's Fair, Seattle, Washington.

Included in "Continuity and Change," Wadsworth Atheneum, Hartford, Connecticut.

Included in "Abstract Drawings and Watercolors: USA," an exhibition organized by The Museum of Modern Art, New York. Shown in Caracas, Rio de Janeiro, São Paulo, Buenos Aires, Montevideo, Santiago, Lima, Guayaquil, Quito, Bogotá, Panama City, and Mexico City.

Included in "Art: USA: Now," the S. C. Johnson & Son, Inc. Collection of Contemporary American Painting shown in Tokyo, London, Athens, Rome, Munich, Monaco, Berlin, Copenhagen, Stockholm, Milan, Brussels, Dublin, Madrid, Lucerne, Paris, Vienna, and throughout the United States, including the Whitney Museum of American Art, New York.

1963

First Louise Lindner Eastman Lecturer in Art, Smith College, Northampton, Massachusetts. Exhibition of thirty paintings at the Smith College Museum of Art. Participates in a symposium on "The Creative Use of the Unconscious by the Artist and by the Psychotherapist" at the Eighth Annual Conference of the American Academy of Psychotherapists at the Waldorf Astoria Hotel, New York City.

Joins the Marlborough-Gerson Gallery, New York City.

Spends the summer in Provincetown.

Visits London and Paris.

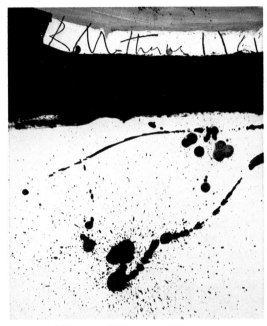

Black and Blue and White. 1961. Oil on paper, sight: 27⅜ x 22½". Collection Mr. and Mrs. David A. Prager, New York.

Exhibition of paintings at the Massachusetts Institute of Technology, Cambridge, Massachusetts.

Included in "Black and White" at the Jewish Museum, New York City.

1964

Paints five mural-size works: *In Green and Ultramarine, Africa I, Africa II, Dublin in 1916, with Black and Tan,* and *Elegy to the Spanish Republic C.*

During the summer in Provincetown collaborates with Bryan Robertson, Director of the Whitechapel Gallery, London on a projected monograph on the artist.

Visits Paris, Venice, and London.

Participates in Seminar on Elementary and Secondary School Education in the Visual Arts at New York University (sponsored by United States Office of Education).

Appointed Visiting Critic at Columbia University's Graduate Program in the Arts in New York City.

Included in "Guggenheim International Award" exhibition at the Solomon R. Guggenheim Museum, New York City, 1964. Winner of a $2,500 prize.

Included in "Paintings from The Museum of Modern Art, New York" at the National Gallery of Art, Washington, D. C.

Included in "Painting & Sculpture of a Decade; 1954-1964," at the Tate Gallery, London.

Included in "American Drawings" at the Solomon R. Guggenheim Museum, New York City.

Included in "Between the Fairs—Twenty-five Years of American Art, 1939-1964" at the Whitney Museum of American Art, New York City.

1965

Interview with Bryan Robertson appears on New York City educational television.

In January writes personal tribute to David Smith.

Exchanges pictures for a sculpture with David Smith.

Retrospective exhibition of collages at the Phillips Collection in Washington, D. C.

Signs several protests organized by the artistic and intellectual community against the war in Vietnam

Participates in a panel discussion on "Cubism and American Painting" at the Solomon R. Guggenheim Museum, New York City. Others participating are Sam Hunter, Robert Rosenblum, and William C. Seitz.

Appointed a director of the College Art Association of America.

Lectures at Bennington College, Bennington, Vermont, at the invitation of Paul Feeley.

Lectures at their request to the graduate students in art at Harvard University, Cambridge, Massachusetts.

Exchanges pictures with Alexander Liberman.

Lectures at the School of Art and Architecture, Yale University, New Haven, Connecticut, at the invitation of Jack Tworkov.

Creates hundreds of small "automatic" pictures in ink on Japanese rice paper in six weeks during the months of April and May. The series is subsequently titled "Lyric Suite."

At the end of May the artist's closest friend, David Smith, dies.

Commissioned to execute mural for J. F. Kennedy Federal Office Building, Boston, Massachusetts designed by The Architects' Collaborative (Walter Gropius, et al.) and Samuel Glaser Associates.

Interviewed on the origins of the Abstract Expressionist movement for *Artforum*.

Appointed Educational Advisor to John Simon Guggenheim Foundation.

Visits Paris, Venice, Dubrovnik, Athens, the Greek Islands, and London during the summer, with his wife and children.

Included in "1943-1953: The Decisive Years," an exhibition of abstract expressionism at the Institute of Contemporary Art, University of Pennsylvania, Philadelphia, Pennsylvania.

Included in "American Collages," an exhibition organized for circulation by The Museum of Modern Art, New York and shown at the Museum during the summer.

Included in "New York School: The First Generation," a major exhibition of paintings of the 1940's and 1950's, organized by the Los Angeles County Museum of Art, Los Angeles, California.

Exhibition "Robert Motherwell: Works on Paper" organized by The Museum of Modern Art, New York for tour of North and South America.

Retrospective exhibition at The Museum of Modern Art, New York; to circulate in Europe in 1966.

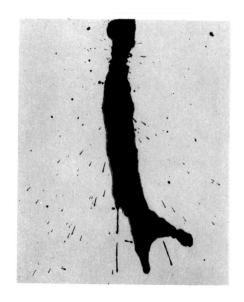

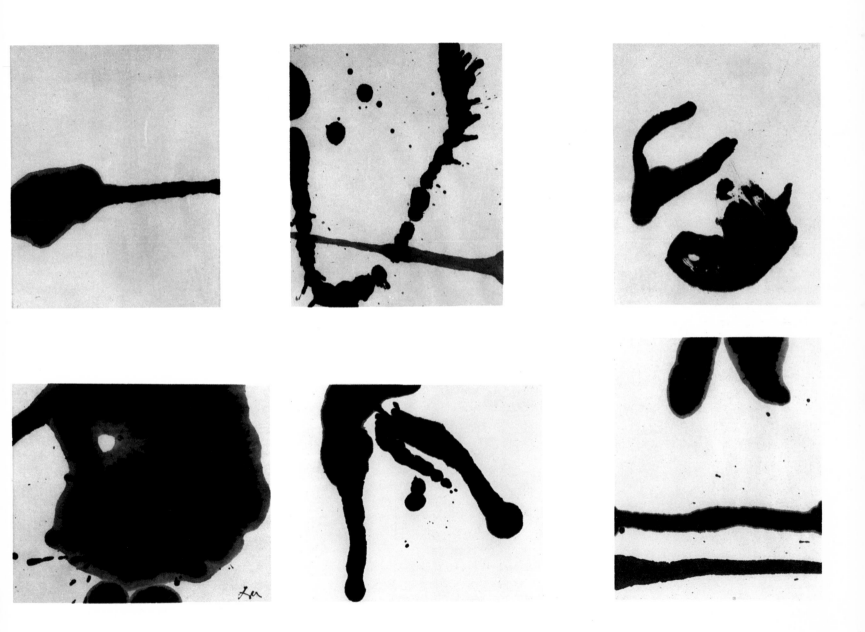

Works from *Lyric Suite*, 1965 .

A Selective Bibliography

At least five long lists on the painter have been published, the first significant and still reliable report being included in Seitz's doctoral dissertation of 1955 (bibl. 84). While these vary in coverage and detail, altogether they cover most of the specific, and in the outstanding instance of Lucy Lippard's comprehensive references on the "New York School," 1965 (bibl. 138), even the general citations on that exciting milieu. Other recent and useful summaries are contained in the 1960 Walker Art Center catalogue (bibl. 139), in the Guggenheim 1961 collective show (bibl. 149) and in the Motherwell Retrospective at Smith College, 1963 (bibl. 151).

These inventories are completed by the major and minor contents of the exhaustive Cuddihy scrapbooks, still in progress (bibl. 47), and certain addenda below, e.g. Namuth (bibl. 74), Portable (bibl. 77), etc. In view of the availability of the bibliographies mentioned above, the present effort, pending a major monograph still in the planning stage, is limited to a classified arrangement of readings selected to support the exhibition and the chronology, to wit: *Writings by the Artist* (nos. 1-38a).—*General Works* (nos. 39-89). — *Articles & Critiques* (nos. 90-132). — *Catalogues & Reviews* (nos. 133-158). Finally, the compiler expresses his appreciation to Elita Taylor of the Library Staff for her valued cooperation on this project.

Bernard Karpel
Librarian of the Museum

Artists' session at Studio 35, 1950, an informal panel discussion on modern art recorded stenographically and printed in part in *Modern Artists in America*, Wittenborn, Schultz, Inc., New York, 1951. Photograph by Max Yavno. Artists participating are:

Upper Photograph, left to right: Lipton, Lewis, Ernst, Grippe, Gottlieb, Hofmann, Barr, Motherwell, Lippold, de Kooning, Lassaw, Brooks, Reinhardt, Pousette-Dart.

Bottom Photograph, left to right: Brooks, Reinhardt, Pousette-Dart, Bourgeois, Ferber, Tomlin, Biala, Goodnough, Sterne, Hare, Newman, Lipton, Lewis, Ernst.

WRITINGS BY THE ARTIST

Includes essays, prefaces, statements, interviews, quotations

1 Notes on Mondrian and Chirico. *VVV* no. 1, p. 59-61 June, 1942.

2 The modern painter's world. *Dyn* v. 1, no. 6, p. 9-14 Nov. 1944.
    Lecture at Mt. Holyoke College, Aug. 10, 1944.

3 Painter's objects. *Partisan Review* v. 11, no 1, p. 93-97 Winter 1944.
    Reprinted partly in bibl. 138.

4 Henry Moore. *New Republic* v. 113, no. 17, p. 538 Oct. 22, 1945.

5 Beyond the aesthetic. *Design* v. 47, no. 8, p. 14-15 Apr. 1946.

6 [Statement]. *In* Fourteen Americans. N. Y., Museum of Modern Art, 1946. *See bibl.* 147.

7 [Statement]. *In* Kootz, Sam, Gallery. Motherwell, May 1947.

8 [Statement] *In* Possibilities: an Occasional Review. N. Y. 1947-48. p. 12.
    Editorial preface with Harold Rosenberg. See bibl. 78.

9 [Prefaces and introductions]. *In* Documents of Modern Art (a series). N. Y., Wittenborn, Schultz (later Wittenborn & Co.), 1947-1955.
    Works by outstanding figures in art and literature, usually translations from European texts. Selected, edited and frequently introduced by Motherwell, e.g. Arp (1948), Ernst (1948), Dada Painters and Poets (1951). For completer details, see bibl. 50.

10 A tour of the sublime. *Tiger's Eye.* v. 1, no. 6, p. 46-47 Dec. 15, 1948.
    In series: The ideas of art, 6 opinions.

11 [Statement]. *In* Kootz, Sam, Gallery. Robert Motherwell Collages 1943-1949. N. Y., 1949. p. 1.
    From Provincetown lecture in *Forum 49* (Mass.), Aug. 11, 1949.

12 [Prefaces]. *In* Kootz, Sam, Gallery. Motherwell, N. Y., Nov. 14-Dec. 4, 1952, p. 2-3. Also: Black or white. N. Y., 1950. p. 2-3.

The latter republished in: Black and white. N. Y., Jewish Museum, 1963. p. 9.

12a The mural. *In* Symbols and inscriptions in the synagogue.
    Millburn, N. J., Congregation B'nai Israel, n.d. (1951?)

13 [Statements]. *Appia Antica* (Rome) no. [1], p. [12] 1959.
    Translations from text "dated" Feb. 10, 1950.

14 The public and the modern artist. *Catholic Art Quarterly* v. 14, p. 80-81 Easter 1951.

15 The School of New York. *In* Paris, Frank, Gallery. Seventeen Modern American Painters. Beverly Hills, Jan. 1951.

16 What abstract art means to me. *Museum of Modern Art Bulletin* v. 18, no. 3, p. 12-13 Spring, 1951.
    Symposium: Calder, Davis, De Kooning, Glarner, Morris, Motherwell (Feb. 5, 1951). Modified text: *Art Digest* v. 25, no. 10, p. 12, 27-28 (Feb. 15, 1951).

17 The rise and continuity of abstract art. *Arts & Architecture* v. 69, no. 9, p. 20-21, 41 Sept. 1951.
    Lecture at the Fogg Museum. Portion printed in: Contemporary American Painting. Urbana, Univ. of Ill, 1952. p. 217.

18 Introduction to the illustrations. *In* Modern Artists in America. N. Y., Wittenborn [1952].
    By the editors: Ad Reinhardt, Robert Motherwell. For details, see bibl. 71. Also [Statement] on end papers.

19 [Joseph Cornell]. Unpublished preface. June 26, 1953. 2 p.
    Prepared for, and in the custody of the Walker Art Center, Minneapolis. Exhibition (July-Aug. 1953) for which a scheduled catalogue did not appear.

20 Is the French avant garde overrated? Art Digest v. 27, p. 13, 27 Sept. 1953.
    Symposium: R. Crawford, C. Greenberg, R. Motherwell, J. Tworkov.

21 The painter and the audience. *Perspectives USA* no. 9, p. 107-112 Autumn 1954.

Symposium on "The creative artist." Portion republished in: The New American Painting. N. Y., Museum of Modern Art, 1959. See bibl. 148.

22 A painting must make human contact. *In* Protter, Eric, ed. Painters on Painting. N. Y., Grosset & Dunlap, 1963.
    From statement in: The New Decade. N. Y., Whitney Museum & Macmillan, 1955. See bibl. 150.

23 [Tomlin]. *In* Bradley Walker Tomlin. N. Y., Whitney Museum of American Art, 1957. p. 11-12.

24 [Statement]. *It is.* no. 3, p. 10, 1959.

25 [T V broadcast: Open End]. N. Y., May 17, 1959.
    On David Susskind panel: "The world of contemporary art." Reported by Genauer (bibl. 103).

26 The significance of Miró. *Art News* v. 58, p. 32-33 May 1959.

27 [The Philadelphia panel on "the concept of the new"]. *It is.* no. 5, p. 35-36 Spring 1960.

28 Painting as self-discovery. London, BBC, Oct. 22, 1960.
    Broadcast title. Changed on publication. See bibl. 32.

29 In support of the French intellectuals. *Partisan Review* Jan.-Feb. 1961.
    A petition about the Algerian war "signed," among many others, by Motherwell.

30 [Letter to Mr. Canaday]. *New York Times* Feb. 26, 1961.
    A protest about his methods of criticism. "Signed," among many others, by Motherwell. Reprinted, in part, in "The Embattled Critic," p. 219-223 (bibl. 46).

31 What should a museum be? *Art in America* no. 2, p. 32-33 1961.
    Reprinted in Pasadena retrospective catalogue, 1962 (bibl. 153).

32 Painting as existence: an interview with Robert Motherwell. *Metro* no. 7, p. 94-97 ill. 1962.
    Conducted by David Sylvester as a BBC broadcast: Painting as self-discovery (London, Oct.

22, 1960). Published with minor revisions and changed title.

33 A conversation at lunch. [1962] *In* Smith College. Robert Motherwell, Northampton, Mass., Jan. 1963.

Notes (3p.) transcribed by Margaret Paul, Nov. 1962.

34 [The deepest identity]. *Newsweek* p. 94 Dec. 10, 1962.

Caption title. Quotes the artist in unsigned article on current Janis show.

35 [Letter to the editor on Esteban Vicente]. *Art News* v. 62, no. 1, p. 6 Mar. 1963.

Reply to Vicente's, v. 61, no. 10, p. 6 Feb. 1963.

36 ["Art, N. Y.": Robert Motherwell interviewed by Bryan Robertson]. N. Y., Dec. 15, 1964.

T V broadcast produced by Colin Clark. Repeated Feb. 18, 1965 on Channel 13. Kinescope in possession of the station.

37 A major American sculptor, David Smith. *Vogue* v. 145, no. 3, p. 135-139, 190-191 Feb. 1, 1965.

38 [Lecture at Yale University. New Haven, Hastings Hall, Apr. 22, 1965].

39p. typescript in possession of the artist. Consists of unrevised transcript of "informal and spontaneous remarks."

38a An interview with Robert Motherwell. *Artforum* v. 4, no. 1, p. 33-37 ill. (col.) Sept. 1965.

Questioner: Max Kozloff.

38b The Motherwell proposal. *In* Conant, Howard, ed. Seminar on Elementary and Secondary School Education in the Arts, N. Y., New York University, 1965. p. 203-209.

Additional quotations, p. 188-189, 202, et passim. Portrait, biography, p. 231.

For additional citations, see Lucy Lippard in the "New York School" (bibl. 138), p. 221-222.

GENERAL WORKS

39 AMERICAN ABSTRACT ARTISTS. The World of Abstract Art. N. Y., Wittenborn, 1957. *p. 165 (index); ill.*

Essays on American painting by Kyle Morris and others.

40 ART SINCE 1945. N. Y., Abrams, 1958. *p. 371 (index)*

American section by Sam Hunter. Also issued as revised paperback.

41 ASHTON, DORE. The Unknown Shore: a View of Contemporary Art. Boston, Toronto, Little, Brown, 1962. *p. 263 (index); ill.*

42 BAUR, JOHN I. H., ed. New Art in America: Fifty Painters of the 20th Century. Greenwich, Conn., New York Graphic Society & Praeger, 1957. *p. 247-248; ill. (col.)*

Text by Frederick Wight.

43 BAYL, FREDERICK. Bilder unser Tage. Cologne, DuMont Schauberg, 1960. *p. 76, 91; ill.*

Quotes from "14 Americans" and "Perspectives USA, no. 9."

44 BERGGRUEN, HEINZ, GALERIE. Robert Motherwell Collages. Paris, Berggruen, 1961. [26]*p. incl. ill. (col.)*

French text (2p.) by Sam Hunter. Translated into Italian (bibl. 155) and English (bibl. 158). Booklet (Collection Berggruen no. 34) issued on the occasion of an exhibition.

45 BLESH, RUDI. Modern Art USA. N. Y., Knopf, 1956. *p. vii (index)*

46 CANADAY, JOHN. Embattled Critic. N.Y., Farrar, Straus and Cudahy, 1962 (c1959). *p. 219-223*

"Views on modern art" reflects New York milieu. Reprints N. Y. Times letter (Feb. 26, 1961) "signed" by Motherwell and others.

47 CUDDIHY, JOHN MURRAY, Compiler. [Scrapbooks on Robert Motherwell]. N. Y., 195? — in progress. 2v.; ill.

A collector's continuing assembly of articles, catalogues, illustrations, clippings, etc. As of 1965, there are two albums, photocopies of which are on deposit in The Museum of Modern Art Library. Includes some items contributed by the artist.

48 CURRENT BIOGRAPHY YEARBOOK. Vol. 23. Editor: Charles Moritz. N. Y., Wilson Co., 1962. *p. 308-310; port.*

49 DIEHL, GASTON. The Moderns: a Treasury of Painting throughout the World. N. Y., Crown [1961]. *p. 210 (index)*

With biography. Translated from the French.

50 DOCUMENTS OF MODERN ART. A Series Edited by Robert Motherwell. N. Y., Wittenborn, Schultz, later Wittenborn & Co., 1947-1955.

On outstanding figures in art and literature, often translated from European texts. Usually with introductions or prefatory notes by Motherwell. These include: *Arp.* On My Way. 1948 (p. 6). — *Ernst.* Beyond Painting. 1948 (p. 5-6).—*Apollinaire.* The Cubist Painters. 1949 (p. 4-5).—*Kahnweiler.* The Rise of Cubism. 1949 (p. 6-8).—*Duthuit.* The Fauvist Painters. 1950 (p. 9-10).—*Raymond.* From Baudelaire to Surrealism. 1950 (p. 1-2).—*The Dada Painters and Poets.* 1951 (p. 11-37).—*Mondrian.* Plastic Art and Pure Plastic Art. 1951 (p. 5-6), etc.

51 ELIOT, ALEXANDER. Three Hundred Years of American Painting. N. Y., Time Inc., 1957. *p. 276-277; ill. (col.)*

52 FAISON, S. LANE, Jr. Art Tours & Detours in New York State. N. Y., Random House, 1964. *p. 23-24, ill.*

53 FLANAGAN, GEORGE A. Understand and Enjoy Modern Art. rev. ed. N. Y., Crowell, 1962 (c.1951). *p. 320*

54 FREEDMAN, LEONARD, ed. Looking at Modern Painting. rev. ed. N. Y., Norton, 1961. *p. 72, 77-79, 84, 126; ill.*

Originally published, under same title, by the Department of Art of the University of California, Los Angeles, 1957.

55 GAUNT, WILLIAM, Compiler. Everyman's Dictionary of Pictorial Art. London, Dent; N. Y., Dutton, 1962. *v. 2, p. 133*

56 GOODRICH, LLOYD & BAUR, JOHN I. H. American Art of Our Century. N. Y., Whitney Museum of American Art & Praeger, 1961. *p. 210, 219; ill.*

57 GREENBERG, CLEMENT. Art and Culture. Boston, Beacon, 1961. *p. 277 (index); ill.*

Includes previously published articles, e.g. *Partisan Review* Spring 1955.

58 GROSSER, MAURICE. The Painter's Eye. N. Y., New American Library, 1961 (c. 1951). *p. 97, 180; ill.*

59 GUGGENHEIM, PEGGY. Confessions of an Art Addict. N. Y., Macmillan, 1960. *p. 104.*

60 HAFTMANN, WERNER. Painting in the Twentieth Century. N. Y., Praeger, 1960. *v. 1, p. 423 (index); v. 2, p. 501 (ill.)*
Revised and translated revision of German edition. (1954-57).

61 HENNING, EDWARD B. Paths of Abstract Art. N. Y., Cleveland Museum of Art, distributed by Abrams, 1960. *p. 36-37; ill.*
Also issued as exhibition catalogue. Nos. 52-54 by Motherwell; biography and critique.

62 HESS, THOMAS B. Abstract Painting: Background and American Phase. N. Y., Viking, 1951. *p. 132, 136-137; ill.*

63 HUNTER, SAM. Modern American Painting and Sculpture. N. Y., Dell, 1959. *p. 254 (index); ill.*
Biography, p. 212. Additional text in *Art Since 1945* (bibl. 40) *Robert Motherwell Collages* (bibl. 152).

64 JANIS, HARRIET & BLESH, RUDI. Collage: Personalities, Concepts, Techniques, N. Y., Philadelphia, Chilton, 1962. *p. 301 (index); ill.*

65 JANIS, SIDNEY. Abstract & Surrealist Art in America. N. Y., Reynal & Hitchcock, 1944. *p. 50-51, 65, 89; ill.*
Brief statement, p. 65.

66 LARKIN, OLIVER W. Art and Life in America. rev. ed. N. Y., Holt, Rinehart & Winston, 1960 (c. 1949). *p. 468, 483, 488; ill.*
LOOKING AT MODERN PAINTING. Los Angeles, 1957. See bibl. 54

67 McCOUBREY, JOHN W. American Tradition in Painting. N. Y., Braziller, 1963. *p. 128 (index): ill.*
Quotes Motherwell briefly (p. 113). General bibliography.

68 MENDELOWITZ, DANIEL M. A History of American Art. N. Y., Holt, Rinehart & Winston, 1960. *p. 601-603; ill.*

69 METRO. International Directory of Contemporary Art. Milan, Editoriale Metro [1963]. *p. 252-253; ill., port.*

70 McDARRAH, FRED W. The Artist's World in Pictures. N. Y., Dutton, 1961. *p. 126 (port.)*

71 MODERN ARTISTS IN AMERICA. First Series. Editorial associates: Robert Motherwell, Ad Reinhardt. Photography: Aaron Siskind. Documentation: Bernard Karpel. N.Y., Wittenborn, Schultz [1951]. 198p. ill.
Preface dated 1951. Sections relevant to Motherwell include: *Introduction to the illustrations* (by the editors).—*Artists' sessions at Studio 35* (quotes Motherwell). — *Statement* (endpapers).

72 MODESTI, RENZO. Pittura Moderna nel Mundo. Milan, Vallardi, 1961. *p. 214, 127; col. ill.*

73 MYERS, BERNARD S., ed. Encyclopedia of Painting. N. Y., Crown, 1955. *p. 353, ill.*

74 NAMUTH, HANS. [Photographs of Robert Motherwell]. [N. Y., etc., 1957-1958].
Approximately 50 negative strips of the artist informally photographed at home and in the studio. Commissioned for a documentary exhibition on the younger American artist at the Brussels World's Fair, 1958. Now deposited for study in the Photo Archive of The Museum of Modern Art Library as a gift from the photographer.

75 NORDNESS, LEE, ed. Art USA Now. Text by Allen S. Weller. N. Y., Viking, 1963. *v. 2, p. 288-291; ill. (col.)*
Essay by Jane Gollin, p. 288-289.

76 PONENTE, NELLO. Modern Painting: Contemporary Trends. [Switzerland, Skira; Cleveland, World Publishers (distributor), 1960]. *p. 76-77, 79, 142, 197; col. ill.*
Biographical and bibliographical note.

77 PORTABLE GALLERY. Robert Motherwell [Colorslides]. N. Y., Portable Gallery [1963-1964?].
42 colorslides in 35 mm., available in cardboard or glass. Additions from time to time. e.g. first edition: 30 slides (1944-1962).

78 POSSIBILITIES. An Occasional Review. No. 1, Winter 1947-48. Only one issue, published by Wittenborn Schultz, N. Y., 1947, in the series "Problems of Contemporary Art." Editors: Robert Motherwell (art), Harold Rosenberg, Pierre Chareau, John Cage. Statement by Motherwell and Rosenberg, p. 74.

79 PROTTER, ERIC, ed. Painters on Painting. N. Y., Grosset & Dunlap, 1963. p. 250.
Statement, 1955: "A painting must make human contact," from *The New Decade* (Whitney Museum, 1955).

80 READ, HERBERT. Art Now. An Introduction to the Theory of Modern Painting and Sculpture. rev. ed. London, Faber & Faber [1948]. *plate 155*

81 RICHARDSON, EDGAR P. A Short History of Painting in America. N. Y., Crowell, 1963. *p. 308*

82 RODMAN, SELDEN. Conversations with Artists. N. Y., Devin-Adair, 1957. *p. 14, 92, 95, 99*

83 ROSENBERG, HAROLD. The Anxious Object: Art Today and Its Audience. N. Y., Horizon, 1964. *p. 26, 101*

84 SEITZ, WILLIAM C. Abstract-Expressionist Painting in America. An Interpretation based on the Work and Thought of Six Key Figures. [Princeton University Dissertation, 1955]. *495p.; ill.*
Typescript. Discusses De Kooning, Gorky, Hofmann, Motherwell, Rothko. Copy on deposit at the Museum of Modern Art Library lacks illustrations. Microfilm available from University Microfilms, Ann Arbor. General bibliography, p. 482 ff. — Motherwell bibliography, 490-493.

85 SEUPHOR, MICHEL. Dictionnaire de la Peinture Abstraite. Paris, Hazan [1957]. *p. 228-229; ill.*
Also English edition: N. Y., Paris Book center [1958?]. Motherwell illustrations (nos. 358, 385) in the author's "Abstract Painting" (N.Y., 1961).

86 SOBY, JAMES THRALL. Contemporary Painters. N. Y., Museum of Modern Art, 1948. *p. 72, 77; ill.*
Reprints essay on "Some Younger American Painters."

87 TEN WORKS—TEN PAINTERS. A Portfolio of Ten

Works by Ten Painters. Hartford, Conn., Wadsworth Atheneum, 1964.
  Silk-screen reproductions selected by Samuel J. Wagstaff, Jr. include one Motherwell. Edition of 500 copies boxed in folio.

87a VOLLMER, HANS. Allgemeines Lexikon der Bildenden Künstler. Leipzig, Seemann, 1956. *v. 3, p. 431*
  Brief bibliography.

88 WEITZ, MORRIS. Philosophy of the Arts. Cambridge, Mass., Harvard University Press, 1950. *p. 88-92*
  Includes text by author and artist on his "The Spanish Prison."

89 WOMEN. A Collaboration of Artists and Writers. N. Y., Kootz Gallery, 1948. *p. 45-47; ill.*
  Based on exhibition, Sept. 1947. Includes reproduction and Weldon Kees: A pastiche for Eve.

ARTICLES & CRITIQUES

90 Alloway, Lawrence. Sign and surface: notes on black and white painting in New York. *Quadrum* no. 9, p. 59-62 ill. 1960.
  Quotes Motherwell. General references.

91 Ashton, Dore. [Motherwell at the Janis Gallery]. *Arts & Architecture* v. 74, no. 7, p. 4 (ill.) July 1957; v. 80, no. 2, p. 8 Feb. 1963.

92 Ashton, Dore. Motherwell loves and believes. *Studio* v. 165, no. 839, p. 116-117 ill. Mar. 1963.
  On "Chi ama, crede" (1962) at the Janis Gallery.

93 Ashton, Dore. Robert Motherwell, passion and transfiguration. *Studio* v. 167, no. 851, p. 100-105 ill. Mar. 1964.
  French, Italian and German summaries.

94 Ashton, Dore. Perspective de la peinture américaine. *Cahiers d'Art* v. 33-35, p. 219-220 ill. 1960.

95 Ashton, Dore. La voix du tourbillon dans l'Amérique de Kafka. *XXe Siècle* new ser., no. 23, p. 92-96 ill. May 1964.
  Also English summary.

96 Berkman, Florence. Motherwell opens art lecture series. *Hartford Times* Mar. 24, 1962.
  Report, p. 26, includes "quotes" from lecture at auditorium of the Burns School.

97 B[ird], P[aul]. Motherwell: a profile. *Art Digest* v. 26, no. 1, p. 6, 23 port. Oct. 1, 1951.

98 Claus, Jurgen. Robert Motherwell—grundtypen series Werkes. *Kunstwerk* v. 18, no. 8, p. 3-9 ill. Feb. 1965.
  Includes "Gespräche mit Robert Motherwell" (4 p.)

99 Deepest identity. *Newsweek* v. 60, no. 24, p. 94 port. Dec. 10, 1962.
  Unsigned article on the occasion of his current Janis show. Quotes the artist frequently.

100 Drudi, Gabriella. Robert Motherwell. *Appia Antica* [no. 1, p. 10-12] ill. 1959.
  Italian text, including statements by the artist (1950).

101 Fitzsimmons, James. Artists put faith in new ecclesiastic art. *Art Digest* v. 26 no. 2, p. 15, 23 ill. Oct. 15, 1951.
  On the Millburn, N. J. synagogue (Gottlieb, Ferber, Motherwell). Similar coverage in *Interiors* v. 111 no. 4, p. 12, 14 ill. Nov. 1951 (Modern Art in a synagogue); *Magazine of Art* v. 44, p. 216 ill. Oct., 1951 (Modern Art for the Millburn Synagogue); *Time* v. 58, p. 87 ill. Nov. 19, 1951 (Signs & symbols).

102 Fitzsimmons, James. Robert Motherwell. *Design Quarterly* no. 29, p. 18-22 ill. (port.) 1954.

103 Genauer, Emily. Arts: T V debate. *New York Herald Tribune* Apr. 24, 1959.
  Comments on David Susskind program: "Open End: the World of Contemporary Art." Announced participants: Genauer, d'Harnoncourt, Shahn, Nordness, Goodrich, Motherwell.

104 Goldwater, Robert. Reflections on the New York school. *Quadrum* no. 8, p. 17-36 ill. 1960.

105 Goosen, Eugene C. Robert Motherwell and the seriousness of subject. *Art International* v. 3, no. 1-2, p. 33-35, 38, 51 ill. 1959.

106 Greenberg, Clement. "American type" painting. *Partisan Review* v. 22, no. 2, p. 179-196 Spring 1955.
  Includes Motherwell in a discussion of abstract expressionism, USA. Reprinted in bibl. Other references in *The Nation*: v. 159, p. 599.—v. 162, p. 110.—v. 164, p. 664-665, etc. 1944-1948.

107 Greenberg, Clement. America takes the lead, 1945-1965. *Art in America* v. 59, no. 4, p. 108-129 ill. Aug.-Sept. 1965.
  Reviews the New York group, with photo of "The Irascible Eighteen" (p. 114-115), and Motherwell in studio (p. 119).

108 Henning, Edward B. Some contemporary paintings. *Cleveland Museum Bulletin* v. 49, p. 50-51 col. ill. Mar. 1962.
  Additional commentary: Language of art. v. 51, p. 217-219 Nov. 1964.

109 Heron, Patrick. The Americans at the Tate Gallery. *Arts* v. 30, p. 15-17 ill. Mar. 1956.
  Includes eulogy of Motherwell, p. 17.

110 Kees, Weldon. Robert Motherwell. *Magazine of Art* v. 41 no. 3, p. 86-88 ill. Mar. 1948.
  For his "A pastiche for Eve," see bibl. 89.

111 Kozloff, Max. Notes on the psychology of modern draughtsmanship. *Arts* v. 38, p. 63 ill. Feb. 1964.

112 Kroll, Jack. American painting and the convertible spiral. *Art News* v. 60, p. 36 ill. Nov. 1961.
  Abstract-expressionists and imagists at the Guggenheim.

113 Lanes, Jerrold. Reflections on post-cubist painting. *Arts* v. 33 no. 8, p. 24-29 ill. May 1959.
  Based on three New York exhibitions (Tàpies, Newman, Motherwell).

114 Langsner, Jules. Art news from Los Angeles [on Motherwell's reception at Pasadena]. *Art News* v. 61, p. 46 May 1962.

115 [Motherwell, art consultant]. *Partisan Review* v. 29 no. 4, p. 593 Fall 1962.
  Announcement: "beginning next issue." Previously, the artist had designed their cover for "Dissonant Voices in Soviet Literature" (no. 3-4, 1961). Resigned, 1965.

116 The Motherwell collections. *Vogue* v. 143, no. 2, p. 88-91, 118 ill. (col.), Jan. 15, 1964.

117 O'Doherty, Brian. Objective works in introspection are displayed at Sidney Janis Gallery. *New York Times* Dec. 6, 1962.

117a O'Hara, Frank. Art Chronicle. *Kulchur* v. 3, no. 9, p. 63 Spring 1963.

118 Ostermann, Robert. Men who lead an American revolution. *National Observer* (London) p. 18 Feb. 17, 1964.
   Includes Motherwell statement.

119 Philadelphia panel. *It Is.* no. 5, p. 34-38 Spring 1960.
   Panel at the Philadelphia Museum of Art, Text edited by P. G. Pavia and Irving Sandler with modifications by the speakers: Guston, Motherwell, Reinhardt, Rosenberg, Tworkov. Subject: Concept of the new. Reviewed by John Canaday, *New York Times* Apr. 3, 1960.

120 Reinhardt, Ad. How to look at modern art in America: 1946-1961. *Art News* v. 60, no. 4, p. 36-37 Summer 1961.
   A very personal "Tree of American art," tracing stylistic and group developments.

121 Rosenberg, Harold. Art in orbit. *Art News* v. 60, p. 22 ill. Oct. 1961.

122 Rosenblum, Robert. Unité et divergences de la peinture américaine. *Aujourd'hui* no. 8, p. 12-18 ill. July 1958.

123 Robert Motherwell. *Bulletin of the Allen Memorial Art Museum* v. 9, no. 3, p. 110-112 ill. Spring 1952.
   Quotes from the "Documents of Modern Art" series. Catalogue lists 17 works.

124 Russell, John. The "new American painting" captures Europe. *Horizon* v. 2, no. 2, p. 41 col. ill. Nov. 1959.

125 Sandler, Irving H. New York letter. *Quadrum* no. 14, p. 116-117 ill. 1963.
   Additional commentary by Sandler: *Art International* v. 5, no. 5-6, p. 43-44 ill. June-Aug. 1961.

126 Sawyer, Kenneth B. The Grossman collection.

Catalogue of first one-man exhibition at Peggy Guggenheim's Art of This Century gallery, 1944.

Studio International v. 169, no. 862, p. 82-87 ill. Feb. 1965.

127 Schuyler, James. Is there an American print revival?—New York. *Art News* v. 60, no. 9, p. 36-37 ill. Jan. 1962.

On the Universal Limited Art Edition.

128 Seitz, William. The rise and dissolution of the avant-garde. *Vogue* v. 142, no. 1, p. 230 ill. Sept. 1, 1963.

129 Seuphor, Michel. Paris-New York 1951. *Art d'Aujourd'hui* v. 2, no. 6, p. 4 ff June 1951.

Special number: La peinture aux Etats-Unis. Includes Motherwell statement on abstract art, p. 21.

130 Sylvester, David. Painting as existence: an interview with Robert Motherwell. *Metro* no. 7 1962. See bibl. 28, 32.

131 Tillim, Sidney. Month in review. [Motherwell at the Janis Gallery]. *Arts* v. 37, no. 4, p. 40-42 ill. Jan. 1963.

131a [Vietnam protest]. *New York Times* Apr. 18, 1965. Motherwell among the signatories. "Writers and Artists" protest coordinated by Mitchell Goodman.

132 Willard, Charlotte. Drawing today. *Art in America* v. 52, no. 5, p. 56 col. ill. Oct. 1964.

CATALOGUES & REVIEWS

For extensive addenda to this selected list, see bibl. 84 (1955), bibl. 139 (1960), bibl. 140 (1951), bibl. 151 (1963), and bibl. 138 (1965). Also note chronology here (p. 73).

133 BENNINGTON COLLEGE. Motherwell. First Retrospective Exhibition. Bennington, Vt., Apr. 24-May 23, 1959.

29 works (1941-1959); portrait; commentary by E. C. Goosen.

134 BRUSSELS. UNIVERSAL AND INTERNATIONAL EXHIBITION. American Art. Apr. 17-Oct. 18, 1958. *p. 66, 75; ill.*

No. 141-144 by Motherwell. Namuth photos on

the Young American Generation (bibl. 74) exhibited on this occasion.

135 CAMBRIDGE. FOGG ART MUSEUM. Modern Painting. Drawing and Sculpture collected by Louise and Joseph Pulitzer, Jr. Cambridge, Mass., 1958. *v. 2, p. 238-239; ill.*

Text by C. S. Cheatham.

136 CLEVELAND. MUSEUM OF ART. Paths of Abstract Art. Cleveland, The Museum & N. Y., Abrams (distributor), 1960. *p. 36-37; ill.*

No. 52-54 by Motherwell (3 ill.). Brief biographical and critical note. Text by Edward B. Henning.

137 KASSEL. MUSEUM FRIDERICIANUM. Documenta II. Cologne, DuMont Schauberg, 1959. *v. 1, p. 284-287; ill.*

Vol. I: *Malerei* includes biography, portrait, colorplate. Exhibited July 11-Oct. 11, 1959.

138 LOS ANGELES. COUNTY MUSEUM OF ART. New York School. The First Generation: Paintings of the 1940's and 1950's. July 16-Aug. 1, 1965. *p. 129-138, 221-223; ill. (col.)*

No. 60-67 by Motherwell. Individual (p. 21) and group statements (p. 33-41) from bibl. 3 and 71 respectively. Outstanding general (p. 209-252) and specific bibliography (p. 221-223) by Lucy Lippard.

139 MINNEAPOLIS. WALKER ART CENTER. 60 American Painters: 1960. Abstract Expressionist Painting of the Fifties. Apr. 3-May 8, 1960. *p. 50-51, 70-71; ill.*

Introduction by H. H. Arnason, organizer of the exhibition. No. 38 by Motherwell; biographical note, bibliography (p. 70-71). General bibliography (p. 54-57). For review see Herbert Read and H. H. Arnason, *Art News* v. 59, p. 32-36 May 1960.

140 MINNEAPOLIS. UNIVERSITY OF MINNESOTA. DEPARTMENT OF ART. 40 American Painters, 1940-1950. June 4-Aug. 30, 1951.

No. 49-50 by Motherwell (2 ill.). Brief statement from Fogg lecture, Apr. 1951.

141 [MOSCOW. AMERICAN NATIONAL EXHIBI-

TION. American Painting and Sculpture. Detroit, Archives of American Art, July 25-Sept. 5, 1959. *Russian text; 100 p.; ill.*

Issued as a printed catalogue in Russian for limited distribution, with a mimeograph supplement (text only) in English. No. 38 by Motherwell, port., ill.; biographical note. Curator of the Moscow exhibition: Edith Gregor Halpert; Asst. Curator, R. V. McLanathan.

142 NEW YORK. ART OF THIS CENTURY. Robert Motherwell. N. Y., Oct.-Nov. 1944.

Preface by J. J. Sweeney. 47 works in many media. Reviewed in *Art Digest* v. 19, p. 16, Nov. 1, 1944; *Art News* v. 43, p. 26 Nov. 1, 1944. Also note bibl. 59.

143 NEW YORK. COORDINATING COUNCIL OF FRENCH RELIEF SOCIETIES. First Papers of Surrealism. Oct. 14-Nov. 7, 1942.

"Hanging" by Breton, "twine" by Duchamp, foreword by Sidney Janis. Reproduces one work by Motherwell. Held at the Whitelaw Reid Mansion.

144 NEW YORK. SIDNEY JANIS GALLERY. [Collective Exhibitions]. N. Y., 1959-1963.

General shows in which Motherwell was represented, usually one work, one illustration: *8 American Painters* (Jan. 5-31, 1959).—*8 Americans* (Apr. 1-20, 1957).—*9 American Painters* (Apr. 4-23, 1960).—*X Years of Janis* (Sept. 29-Nov. 1, 1958).—*11 Abstract Expressionist Painters* (Oct. 7-Nov. 2, 1963), etc.

145 NEW YORK. SIDNEY JANIS GALLERY. [Robert Motherwell Catalogues]. N. Y., 1957-1962.

1. Paintings and collages. May 13-June 8, 1957. Reviews: *Art News* v. 56, p. 21 June 1, 1957; *Arts & Architecture* v. 74, p. 4 July 1957; *Arts* v. 31, p. 56 Sept. 1957; *New York* v. 33, p. 86 June 1, 1957.

2. Motherwell. Mar. 9-Apr. 4, 1958. Reviews: *Art News* v. 58 p. 10 Apr. 1959; *Arts* v. 33, p. 53 Apr. 1959, p. 28-29 May 59; *Arts & Architecture* v. 76, p. 7-8 May 1959.

3. Recent Paintings and Collages. Apr. 10-May 6, 1961. 20 p. incl. port., 21 ill. Lists 26 works.

Review: *Art News* v. 60, p. 10 May, 1961; *Arts* v. 35, p. 84 May 1961.

4. New Paintings in Oil and Collage. Dec. 4-29, 1962. 28 ill. Reviews: *Art International* v. 7, no. 1, p. 68-69; *Art News* v. 61, p. 10 Jan. 1963; *Arts* v. 37, p. 40-42 Jan. 1963; *Arts & Architecture* v. 80, p. 8 Feb. 1963.

146 NEW YORK. SAM KOOTZ GALLERY. [Motherwell Exhibitions]. N. Y., 1946-1953.

These include: *Paintings, Collages, Drawings.* Jan. 2-19, 1946 and subsequent annual exhibitions (omitting 1951?) through *Paintings, Collages, Drawings. Apr. 6-25, 1953.* Reviews in magazines for Jan. 1946, May 1947, June 1948, Oct. 1949, Dec. 1950, Apr. 1952, Apr. 1953, etc. are listed in the Walker and Smith catalogues (bibl. 139, 151). In addition Motherwell has been represented in many group shows, among which are: The Big Top (Mar. 1-23, 1946).— Black or White (Feb. 28-Mar. 1950). Preface by the artist.—Building a Museum Collection (May 13-June 1, 1946).— A Decade of Modern Painting and Sculpture (Apr. 11-May 7, 1955). —French and American Painting and Sculpture (Mar. 29-Apr. 17, 1948).—Homage to Jazz (Dec. 3-21, 1946).—In the Sun (Sept. 4-28, 1946).— The Muralist and the Modern Architect (Oct. 3-23, 1950) "The muralist: Robert Motherwell". —Résumé of the 1950-51 Season (June 4-29, 1951), etc.

147 NEW YORK. MUSEUM OF MODERN ART. Fourteen Americans. Sept. 10-Dec. 8 1946. *p. 34-38, 78; ill.*

Catalogue and exhibition by Dorothy C. Miller. Statements by the Artists. Nos. 57-69 by Motherwell (6 ill.). Biography. Some general exhibitions including this artist are: *Abstract Painting and Sculpture* (1951).—*The Art of Assemblage* (1961).—*American Collages* (1965). One-man circulating show (with catalogue and bibliography) 1965-1967.

148 NEW YORK. MUSEUM OF MODERN ART. INTERNATIONAL PROGRAM. The New American Painting as Shown in Eight European Countries 1958-1959. N. Y., The Museum, 1959. *p. 56-59, 92-93; ill. (col.)*

Preface by A. H. Barr, Jr. Organized by Porter McCray. No. 45-49 by Motherwell. Statement by Motherwell from *Perspectives USA* (bibl. 21). Catalogues issued in different languages and format as the show circulated in Basel, Milan, Madrid, Berlin, Amsterdam, Brussels, Paris, London.

149 NEW YORK. SOLOMON R. GUGGENHEIM MUSEUM. American Abstract Expressionists and Imagists. Oct., 1961. *p. 23, 27-28, 62-63, 92, 120; ill.*

Text by H. H. Arnason. No. 41 by Motherwell. Biographical note and bibliography. Motherwell also represented in their: *Younger American Painters:* May 12-July 25, 1954. p. 36-37; *ill.—Guggenheim International Award 1964.* p. 119. General bibliography.—*American Drawings, 1964.* No. 80-83 by Motherwell. Bibliography.

150 NEW YORK. WHITNEY MUSEUM OF AMERICAN ART. The New Decade: 35 American Painters and Sculptors. 1955-56. p. 58-59, 94, ill. Includes Motherwell statement and documentation. Exhibit circulated: San Francisco, Los Angeles (Univ. of Cal.), Colorado Springs, St. Louis.

151 NORTHAMPTON. SMITH COLLEGE. MUSEUM OF ART. An Exhibition of the Work of Robert Motherwell. Northampton, Mass., Jan. 10-28, 1963. *32 p., ill.*

30 exhibits (15 ill.). Motherwell texts, chronology, extensive bibliography (with addenda slip). Announcement: "to accompany the first Louise Lindner Eastman memorial lecture."

152 PARIS. GALERIE BERGGRUEN. Robert Motherwell Collages. [Fall] 1961.

Reviewed in *Aujourd'hui* v. 6, p. 30 Oct. 1961. Booklet issued as catalogue and on the occasion of the exhibit. (See bibl. 44). Hunter text reprinted in bibl. 155, 158.

153 PASADENA ART MUSEUM. Robert Motherwell,

a Retrospective Exhibition. Feb. 18-Mar. 11, 1962. *28 p., ill.*

Texts by T. W. Leavitt, Frank O'Hara, Sam Hunter, poem by Barbara Guest, essay by the artist. Reviewed: *Art News* v. 61, p. 46 May, 1962; *Arts* v. 36, p. 50 Feb. 1962; *Craft Horizons* v. 22, p. 41 July 1962.

154 PITTSBURGH. CARNEGIE INTERNATIONAL. [Annuals]. 1952-1964.

Motherwell included in 1952 (no. 187), 1955 (no. 207), 1958 (no. 311), 1964-65 (no. 348).

155 ROME. ODYSSIA GALLERIES. Collages di Motherwell. Rome, Jan. 1962. *[12] p., ill. (col.)*

28 works (7 ill.). Hunter text translated from bibl. 44.

156 SAO PAULO. MUSEU DE ARTE MODERNA. VI BIENAL. Estades Unidos. 1961. *p. [5-11], ill. (col.)*

Section organized by the Museum of Modern Art. Bilingual text by Frank O'Hara. Lists 27 paintings, 6 drawings. Also: Catálogo geral. (1961), p. 186-191. In addition, Motherwell represented in *II Bienal,* Dec. 1953 (no. 11-15, p. 150), and *VII Bienal,* Sept.-Dec. 1963 (no. 24-26).

157 URBANA. UNIVERSITY OF ILLINOIS. COLLEGE OF FINE & APPLIED ARTS. 12th Exhibition of Contemporary American Painting and Sculpture. Mar. 7-Apr. 11, 1965.

Exhibited no. 91 (ill. p. 44). Documentation (p. 45). Motherwell also represented in the 1949 annual (pl. 13, biography).—1950 annual (pl. 30, biography).—1953 (pl. 83, biography).— 1955 (pl. 2, biography).

158 WASHINGTON. PHILLIPS COLLECTION. Collages by Robert Motherwell. Washington, D.C., Jan. 2-Feb. 15, 1965. *12 p., ill. (port.)*

30 examples. includes translation of Hunter preface (bibl. 44).

Catalogue

The artist dedicates the exhibition to his wife, Helen Frankenthaler

New York showing: September 30-November 28, 1965. The exhibition will travel in Europe during 1966 under the auspices of the International Council of The Museum of Modern Art.
Dates enclosed in parentheses do not appear on the works. In dimensions height precedes width. Works marked with an asterisk are illustrated.

*1 *The Red Sun*. (1941). Ink and oil on cardboard, 8⅛ x 10″. Collection Mr. and Mrs. William Boss-chart, Hillsborough, California. Ill. p. 96.

2 *Collage*. 1943. Collage, 19¾ x 14⅛″. Collection Mme. Pierre Chareau, New York.

*3 *The Joy of Living*. 1943. Collage, sight: 43½ x 35¼″. The Baltimore Museum of Art, Baltimore, Maryland, Saidie A. May Collection. Ill. p. 20.

*4 *Pancho Villa, Dead and Alive*. 1943. Gouache and oil with collage on cardboard, 28 x 35⅞″. The Museum of Modern Art, New York. Ill. p. 14.

*5 *Collage in Beige and Black*. 1944. Collage on cardboard, 43⅜ x 29⅛″. Collection Ivan von Auw, Jr., New York. Ill. p. 20.

*6 *The Little Spanish Prison*. 1941-44. Oil on canvas, 27⅛ x 17″. Collection the artist. Ill. p. 16.

*7 *Spanish Prison (Window)*. 1943-44. Oil on canvas, 52¼ x 42¼″. Collection Mrs. H. Gates Lloyd, Haverford, Pennsylvania. Ill. p. 12.

*8 *View From a High Tower*. 1944. Collage and oil, sight: 29¼ x 29¼″. Collection Paul Peters, New York. Ill. p. 12.

*9 *Wall Painting with Stripes*. 1944. Oil on canvas, 54 x 67⅛″. Collection J. Patrick Lannan, Chicago, Illinois. Ill. p. 28.

*10 *Figuration*. 1945. Oil on canvas, 18¼ x 14⅛″. Collection Mr. and Mrs. Gifford Phillips, Washington, D. C. Ill. p. 16.

*11 *Viva*. 1946. Oil and collage on canvas, 13 x 16¾″. Collection Dr. Robert E. Kantor, Atherton, California. Ill. p. 16.

*12 *Mallarmé's Swan*. 1944-47. Collage, sight: 43⅝ x 35⅜″. Contemporary Collection of The Cleveland Museum of Art, Cleveland, Ohio. Ill. p. 13.

*13 *Western Air*. 1946-47. Oil on canvas, 72 x 54″. The Museum of Modern Art, New York. Ill. p. 13.

*14 *Emperor of China*. 1947. Oil on canvas, 48 x 36″. The Chrysler Art Museum of Provincetown, Provincetown, Massachusetts. Ill. p. 17.

*15 *In Grey with Parasol*. 1947. Oil and collage on board, sight: 47½ x 35½″. The Art Gallery of Toronto, Toronto, Canada. Ill. p. 21.

*16 *Personage with Yellow Ochre and White*. 1947. Oil on canvas, 72 x 54″. The Museum of Modern Art, New York, gift of Mr. and Mrs. Samuel M. Kootz. *New York only*. Ill. p. 24.

*17 *The Poet*. 1947. Collage, sight: 55⅝ x 39⅛″. Collection Mr. and Mrs. Mark Rothko, New York. *New York only*. Ill. p. 17.

*18 *The Elegy*. 1948. Collage, sight: 29½ x 23½″. Fogg Art Museum, Harvard University, Cambridge, Massachusetts, Louise E. Bettens Fund. Ill. p. 15.

*19 *Elegy to the Spanish Republic I*. (1948). Ink on paper, sight: 10½ x 8⅛″. Collection the artist. Ill. p. 76.

*20 *The Homely Protestant*. (1948). Oil on composition board, 96 x 48″. Collection the artist. Ill. p. 19.

*21 *At Five in the Afternoon*. 1949. Casein on cardboard, 15 x 20″. Collection the artist. Ill. p. 36.

*22 *Collage (In Yellow and White With Torn Elements)*. 1949. Collage, sight: 47⅜ x 35½″. Collection Mr. and Mrs. Ben Heller, New York. *New York only*. Ill. p. 21.

*23 *The Voyage*. (1949). Oil and tempera on paper mounted on composition board, 48 x 94″. The Museum of Modern Art, New York, gift of Mrs. John D. Rockefeller 3rd. Ill. p. 27.

*24 *Interior with Nude*. (1952). Oil on board, 9 x 12″. Collection Mrs. Eleanor Ward, New York. Ill. p. 62.

*25 *Elegy to the Spanish Republic XXXIV*. 1953-54. Oil on canvas, 80 x 100″. Albright-Knox Art Gallery, Buffalo, New York, gift of Seymour H. Knox. *New York only*. Ill. p. 34.

*26 *Fishes with Red Stripe*. 1954. Oil on paper, 42½ x 41⅛″. Collection John Murray Cuddihy, New York. Ill. p. 80.

*27 *Wall Painting IV*. 1954. Oil on canvas, 54⅛ x 72⅛″. Collection Mr. and Mrs. Ben Heller, New York. *New York only*. Ill. p. 43.

*28 *Je t'aime IIa*. 1955. Oil on canvas, 71⅞ x 53¼″. Collection Mr. and Mrs. I. Donald Grossman, New York. Ill. p. 38.

*29 *Je t'aime IV*. 1955-57. Oil on canvas, 70⅛ x 100″. Collection Mr. and Mrs. Walter Bareiss, Munich, Germany. Ill. p. 38.

30 *Helen's Collage*. 1957. Collage, 30 x 19⅝″. Collection Miss Helen Frankenthaler, New York.

*31 *Jour la Maison, Nuit la Rue*. (1957). Oil on canvas, 69¾ x 89⅝″. Collection Mr. and Mrs. William C. Janss, Palm Desert, California, Ill. p. 63.

*32 *The Tearingness of Collaging*. 1957. Collage, sight: 29⅝ x 21⅜″. Collection Mr. and Mrs. Max M. Zurier, Beverly Hills, California. Ill. p. 22.

33 *Iberia No. 2* (1958). Oil on canvas, 47⅛ x 80¼″. Collection the artist.

34 *Iberia No. 5*. (1958). Oil on board, 24¼ x 19⅝″. Collection Mr. and Mrs. Arthur Ross, New York.

*35 *Iberia No. 18*. (1958). Oil on canvas, 5⅛ x 7⅛″. Collection the artist. Ill. p. 62.

*36 *Madrid No. 1* (1958). Crayon and ink on paper, 15¼ x 24¼″. Collection Professor and Mrs. Robert Gutman, Princeton, New Jersey. Ill. p. 62.

*37 *Madrid No. 6*. (1958). Crayon and ink on paper, 15¾ x 17½″. Collection the artist. Ill. p. 62.

*38 *Pink Nude with Bowed Head*. 1958. Oil on paper mounted on cardboard, 23⅞ x 19½″. Collection Miss Helen Frankenthaler, New York. Ill. p. 80.

*39 *A Spanish Elegy*. 1958. Oil on paper, 11½ x 14½″. Collection Mr. and Mrs. Bernard J. Reis, New York. Ill. p. 62.

*40 *Spanish Painting with the Face of a Dog*. (1958). Oil on muslin, 37⅛ x 75¼″. Collection Mr. and Mrs. Gifford Phillips, Washington, D. C. Ill. p. 11.

41 *Two Figures #11*. 1958. Oil on board, 8⅝ x 10⅝″. Collection the artist.

*42 *A View #1*. 1958. Oil on canvas, 81⅛ x 104″. Collection John Murray Cuddihy, New York. Ill. p. 29.

*43 *The Black Sun*. 1959. Oil on paper, sight: 28½ x 22½″. Collection the artist, courtesy of the Marlborough-Gerson Gallery, New York. Ill. p. 30.

44 *Greek Collage*. 1959. Collage, 23¾ x 22¾″. Collection the artist, courtesy of the Marlborough-Gerson Gallery, New York.

*45 *N.R.F. Collage #1*. 1959. Oil and collage, sight: 28½ x 22½″. Whitney Museum of American Art, New York, gift of the Friends of the Whitney Museum. Ill. p. 64.

*46 *Elegy to the Spanish Republic LV*. 1955-60. Oil on canvas, 70⅛ x 76⅛″. Contemporary Collection of The Cleveland Museum of Art, Cleveland, Ohio. Ill. p. 47.

*47 *Elegy to the Spanish Republic LVII*. 1957-60. Oil on canvas, 84 x 108⅞″. Collection Mr. and Mrs. Gardner Hempel, Littleton, Colorado. Ill. p. 66.

*48 *The Figure 4 on an Elegy*. 1960. Oil on paper, 22⅞ x 28¾″. Collection H. H. Arnason, New York. Ill. p. 31.

*49 *The French Line*. (1960). Collage, 30 x 23″. Collection Mr. and Mrs. Sam Hunter, New York. Ill. p. 56.

*50 *In Brown and White*. 1960. Collage, sight: 39½ x 26″. Collection Mr. and Mrs. Joseph S. Iseman, New York. Ill. p. 39.

*51 *N.R.F. Collage #2*. 1960. Collage, sight: 28⅜ x 21½″. Whitney Museum of American Art, New York, gift of the Friends of the Whitney Museum. Ill. p. 64.

*52 *Summertime in Italy #8*. 1960. Oil on canvas, 100⅜ x 70⅜″. Collection the artist, courtesy of Marlborough-Gerson Gallery, New York. Ill. p. 69.

*53 *Two Figures with Cerulean Blue Stripe*. 1960. Oil on canvas, 84 x 109¼″. Collection Sophie and Boris Leavitt, Hanover, Pennsylvania, courtesy of The Baltimore Museum of Art. Ill. p. 52.

*54 *White Collage with Black Stripe*. 1960. Collage, sight: 28⅜ x 22½″. Collection J. Daniel Weitzman, New York. Ill. p. 22.

*55 *Black and Blue and White*. 1961. Oil on paper, sight: 27⅜ x 22½″. Collection Mr. and Mrs. David A. Prager, New York. Ill. p. 83.

*56 *Black on White*. 1961. Oil on canvas, 78 x 162¾″. The Museum of Fine Arts, Houston, Texas. *New York only*. Ill. p. 55.

*57 *Elegy to the Spanish Republic LIV*. 1957-61. Oil on canvas, 70 x 90¼″. The Museum of Modern Art, New York, anonymous gift. Ill. p. 44.

*58 *Elegy to the Spanish Republic LVIII*. 1957-61. Oil on canvas, 84 x 108¾″. Rose Art Museum, Brandeis University, Waltham, Massachusetts, gift of Julian J. and Joachim Jean Aberbach. Ill. p. 46.

*59 *Elegy to the Spanish Republic LXX*. (1961). Oil on canvas, 69 x 114″. Collection the artist, courtesy of Marlborough-Gerson Gallery, New York. Ill. p. 44.

*60 *In Black with Yellow Ochre*. 1961. Oil on paper, 28⅜ x 22⅜″. Collection Mrs. Bliss Parkinson, New York. Ill. p. 31.

*61 *Pyrenean Collage*. (1961). Oil and collage on paper, 23 x 29″. Collection Miss Helen Frankenthaler, New York. Ill. p. 31.

*62 *Summertime in Italy, #7—In Golden Ochre*. 1961. Oil on canvas, 85 x 69⅛″. Collection the artist, courtesy of Marlborough-Gerson Gallery, New York. Ill. p. 69.

*63 *Beside the Sea, #1*. (1962). Oil on paper, 28⅞ x 23½″. Collection Sophie and Boris Leavitt, Hanover, Pennsylvania. Ill. p. 32.

64 *Beside the Sea, #3*. 1962. Oil on paper, 28¾ x 22¾″. Collection the artist, courtesy of Marlborough-Gerson Gallery, New York.

*65 *Beside the Sea, #4*. (1962). Oil on paper, 28⅞ x 23″. Collection Sophie and Boris Leavitt, Hanover, Pennsylvania. Ill. p. 32.

*66 *Beside the Sea, #8*. 1962. Oil on paper, 28⅞ x 22¾″. Collection the artist, courtesy of Marlborough-Gerson Gallery, New York. Ill. p. 32.

*67 *Beside the Sea, #12*. 1962. Oil on paper, 28¾ x 22¾″. Collection the artist, courtesy of Marlborough-Gerson Gallery, New York.

*68 *Beside the Sea, #18*. 1962. Oil on paper, 29 x 23″. Collection Sophie and Boris Leavitt, Hanover, Pennsylvania. Ill. p. 33.

*69 *Beside the Sea, #22*. 1962. Oil on paper, 28¾ x 22¾″. Collection the artist, courtesy of Marlborough-Gerson Gallery, New York. Ill. p. 33.

*70 *Beside the Sea, #24*. 1962. Acrylic on paper, 28¾ x 22¾″. Collection the artist, courtesy of Marlborough-Gerson Gallery, New York. Ill. p. 33.

*71 *Chi Ama, Crede*. 1962. Oil on canvas, 84 x 141″. Collection the artist, courtesy of Marlborough-Gerson Gallery, New York. Ill. p. 57.

72 *Cambridge Collage*. 1963. Oil and paper on board, 40 x 27⅛″. Collection the artist, courtesy of Marlborough-Gerson Gallery, New York.

*73 *Elegy to the Spanish Republic C*. 1963. Oil on canvas, 84 x 240″. Collection the artist, courtesy of Marlborough-Gerson Gallery, New York. Ill. p. 6-7.

*74 *The Magic Skin (Peau de Chagrin)*. 1963. Oil and collage on cardboard, 39¾ x 26⅞″. Yale University Art Gallery, New Haven, Connecticut, gift of the artist. Ill. p. 64.

75 *Summertime in Italy, #10*. 1963. Oil on canvas, 96¼ x 72¼″. Collection the artist, courtesy of Marlborough-Gerson Gallery, New York.

*76 *Throw of Dice, #17*. 1963. Oil on canvas, 72⅛ x 48⅛″. Collection Mr. and Mrs. Robert H. Shoenberg, St. Louis, Missouri. *New York only*. Ill. p. 68.

*77 *Dublin 1916, with Black and Tan*. 1964. Acrylic and oil on canvas, 84⅛ x 204¼″. Collection the artist, courtesy of Marlborough-Gerson Gallery, New York. Ill. p. 48.

*78 *In Blue and White with Calligraphy*. 1964. Collage, 30 x 22″. Collection the artist, courtesy of Marlborough-Gerson Gallery, New York. Ill. p. 41.

*79 *Indian Summer, #1*. 1962-64. Oil and acrylic on canvas, 70⅛ x 63″. Collection Kenneth Noland, South Shaftsbury, Vermont. Ill. p. 65.

*80 *Indian Summer, #2.* 1962-64. Oil and acrylic on canvas, 66⅛ x 50⅛". Collection the artist, courtesy of Marlborough-Gerson Gallery, New York. Ill. p. 65.

81 *In White with Black Ring.* 1964. Ink and collage on cardboard, 30 x 22". Collection the artist, courtesy of Marlborough-Gerson Gallery, New York.

*82 *In White with Pink and Black Rings.* 1964. Collage, 30⅛ x 22". Collection the artist, courtesy of Marlborough-Gerson Gallery, New York. Ill. p. 41.

*83 *In White with 4 Corners.* 1964. Collage on cardboard, 30 x 22". Collection the artist, courtesy of Marlborough-Gerson Gallery, New York. Ill. p. 41.

*84 *In Green and Ultramarine.* 1963-65. Oil on canvas, 88 x 248½". Collection the artist, courtesy of Marlborough-Gerson Gallery, New York. Ill. p. 49.

*85 *Africa.* 1964-65. Acrylic on canvas, 81 x 222½". The Baltimore Museum of Art, Baltimore, Maryland, gift of the artist. Ill. p. 60-61.

86 *Elegy to the Spanish Republic CII.* 1965. Acrylic on canvas, 81¾ x 122⅜". Collection Mr. and Mrs. Robert B. Mayer, Winnetka, Illinois.

*87 *Irish Elegy.* 1965. Acrylic on canvas, 69⅜ x 83¾". Collection the artist, courtesy of Marlborough-Gerson Gallery, New York. Ill. p. 71.

H. H. Arnason, New York; Ivan von Auw, Jr., New York; Mr. and Mrs. Walter Bareiss, Munich, Germany; Mr. and Mrs. William Bosschart, Hillsborough, California; Mme. Pierre Chareau, New York; John M. Cuddihy, New York; Miss Helen Frankenthaler, New York; Mr. and Mrs. I. Donald Grossman, New York; Prof. and Mrs. Robert Gutman, Princeton, New Jersey; Mr. and Mrs. Ben Heller, New York; Mr. and Mrs. Gardiner Hempel, Littleton, Colorado; Mr. and Mrs. Sam Hunter, New York; Mr. and Mrs. Joseph S. Iseman, New York; Mr. and Mrs. William C. Janss, Palm Desert, California; Dr. Robert E. Kantor, Atherton, California; J. Patrick Lannan, Chicago, Illinois; Boris and Sophie Leavitt, Hanover, Pennsylvania; Mrs. H. Gates Lloyd, Haverford, Pennsylvania; Mr. and Mrs. Robert B. Mayer, Winnetka, Illinois; Robert Motherwell, New York; Kenneth Noland, South Shaftsbury, Vermont; Mrs. Bliss Parkinson, New York; Paul Peters, New York; Mr. and Mrs. Gifford Phillips, Washington, D.C.; Mr. and Mrs. David A. Prager, New York; Mr. and Mrs. Bernard J. Reis, New York; Mr. and Mrs. Arthur Ross, New York; Mr. and Mrs. Mark Rothko, New York; Mr. and Mrs. Robert H. Shoenberg, St. Louis, Missouri; Mrs. Eleanor Ward, New York; J. Daniel Weitzman, New York; Mr. and Mrs. Max Zurier, Beverly Hills, California.

Albright-Knox Art Gallery, Buffalo, New York; The Art Gallery of Toronto, Toronto, Canada; The Baltimore Museum of Art, Baltimore, Maryland; Brandeis University, Waltham, Massachusetts; The Chrysler Art Museum of Provincetown, Provincetown, Massachusetts; The Cleveland Museum of Art, Cleveland, Ohio; Fogg Art Museum, Cambridge, Massachusetts; Museum of Fine Arts of Houston, Houston, Texas; The Museum of Modern Art, New York; Whitney Museum of American Art, New York; Yale University Art Gallery, New Haven, Connecticut.

Marlborough-Gerson Gallery, New York.

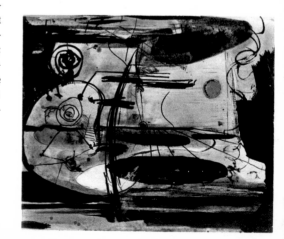

The Red Sun. (1941). Ink and oil on cardboard, 8⅛ x 10". Collection Mr. and Mrs. William Bosschart, Hillsborough, California.